103

BADMINTON

BADMINTON

MASTERING THE BASICS WITH THE PERSONALIZED SPORTS INSTRUCTION SYSTEM

Michael Metzler
Georgia State University

Allyn and Bacon

Boston   London   Toronto   Sydney   Tokyo   Singapore

VICE PRESIDENT	Paul A. Smith
Publisher	Joseph E. Burns
EDITORIAL ASSISTANT	Annemarie Kennedy
MARKETING MANAGER	Rick Muhr
EDITORIAL PRODUCTION SERVICE	Bernadine Richey Publishing Services
TEXT DESIGN AND COMPOSITION	Barbara Bert Silbert
MANUFACTURING BUYER	Julie McNeill
COVER ADMINISTRATOR	Brian Gogolin

Internet: www.abacon.com

ISBN: 0-205-32369-3

Printed in the United States of America

10 9 8 7 6 5 4 3 2 1   05 04 03 02 01 00

CONTENTS

Preface   vii

MODULE 1 **STRETCHING FOR BADMINTON**   1

MODULE 2 **BADMINTON BASICS**   7
    EQUIPMENT   7
    COURT AND NET   8
    BADMINTON FUNDAMENTALS   10
    BASICS OF BADMINTON SHOT MAKING   11
    SHOT MAKING FUNDAMENTALS   22

MODULE 3 **SERVING**   25
    LOW SHORT SERVE   27
    HIGH DEEP SERVE   35

MODULE 4 **CLEARS**   49
    FOREHAND DRIVE CLEAR   49
    BACKHAND DRIVE CLEAR   55
    OVERHEAD CLEAR   61

MODULE 5   **DRIVE SHOTS**   **71**
            FOREHAND DRIVE   71
            BACKHAND DRIVE   77

MODULE 6   **OVERHEAD SMASHES**   **85**

MODULE 7   **DROP SHOTS**   **93**
            FOREHAND DROP   93
            BACKHAND DROP   100

MODULE 8   **LAWS OF BADMINTON AND
            GAME STRATEGY**   **109**
            LAWS OF BADMINTON   111
            BADMINTON STRATEGY   123
            BADMINTON KNOWLEDGE AND STRATEGY QUIZ   127

            **Personal Progress Chart
            for PSIS Badminton**   **vii**

PREFACE

INTRODUCTION TO PSIS BADMINTON

Hello, and welcome to your **badminton class**! That's right, *your* badminton class. This personal workbook includes almost everything you will need to learn the game of badminton and become a proficient beginning-level player. Of course, your instructor will play an important part as you progress, but most of what you will need is contained in your Personal Workbook. Your badminton class will be taught this term using the **Personalized Sports Instruction System (PSIS)**, developed specifically for college basic instruction courses like the one in which you are enrolled. All of the materials in this workbook have been refined in field tests with many students like yourself, college men and women getting their first formal badminton instruction.

The key design feature of the PSIS is that it permits for individualized learning and progression through the course. Think back to other classes you have taken; some students learn faster than others. This is a fact in all learning situations. Depending on individual learning rates, some students become frustrated if the course goes too fast. Others become bored if the course goes too slowly. Either way, many students become disinterested, reducing their enjoyment of the course. For badminton, the most harmful result of frustration or boredom is that students are not given a proper chance to learn the game and to enjoy it as a regular part of their activity schedule. Whether you are a "bare beginner" or currently have some badminton experience, the PSIS design will allow you to progress **"as quickly as you can, or as slowly as you need."** Keep this little motto in mind as you become familiar with this workbook and progress through your badminton class this term.

Another point to keep in mind is that the PSIS is *achievement oriented*. That means the PSIS design is intended to help you learn the necessary skills, strategies, and rules for beginning badminton play. I guarantee you will be a better player at the end of your PSIS class than you are now!

As you will see, your improvement will come in a way that is different from most other courses you have taken. You will be asked to assume more responsibility for your own learning than ever before. Remember, all the instructional material is included in your Personal Workbook. It will be up to you to learn the contents of the workbook, become familiar with the PSIS system, attend class regularly, follow your instructor's class policies, and work diligently toward completing the course sequences. It has been my experience that college students enjoy taking a large role in their own learning and appreciate the individualized plan of the PSIS. I know that you will, too.

ADVANTAGES OF THE PSIS FOR YOU

1. **The PSIS reduces your dependence on the instructor.** Your Personal Workbook provides nearly all the information you will need to complete the course. All content, learning task, and managerial information is at your fingertips, not with the instructor. When you are ready for a new learning task, the individualized plan will allow you to proceed on your own.
2. **Individualized learning is emphasized.** The PSIS will allow you to learn badminton "as quickly as you can, or as slowly as you need." You will be able to remain in your own comfort zone while progressing through the course.
3. **You will have increased responsibility for your own learning.** As adult learners, college students can assume responsibility for much of their own learning. You can make decisions that have direct bearing on class attendance, practice routines, and achievement. The PSIS system shifts much of the responsibility and decision making directly to you and away from the instructor.
4. **Your access to the instructor will be increased whenever you need it.** Since PSIS instructors can spend much more time in class teaching students, it means that you will get more personal attention and quality instruction, *that is, if you need it.* If you do not require as much interaction with the instructor, it will not be forced on you as with group learning strategies.
5. **You can chart your own progress.** Your PSIS Badminton Personal Workbook includes a simple **Personal Progress Chart** to help you gauge your learning as you go through the course. This will help you to make decisions about your learning pace, projected grade, and how to use your class time most efficiently.

YOUR ROLE IN PSIS BADMINTON

Your role in PSIS Badminton can be summarized easily: become familiar with and follow the Personal Workbook as an independent learning guide. You will not need to depend on the instructor for content and managerial information. But when the workbook is not sufficient or specific learning information is needed, you should be sure to *ASK FOR HELP*! Your Personal Workbook will provide nearly all the information needed to complete the course. So, if you can progress without the instructor's direction, the system is designed to let you. If you need help, the instructor will be free to provide it for you. Your instructor will show you a *help signal* for getting his or her attention in class. It might be a raised hand, a raised racquet, or a verbal call. Be sure you know this signal, and do not be shy about using it!

YOUR INSTRUCTOR'S ROLE IN PSIS BADMINTON

Your instructor has the important role of *facilitator* in your PSIS badminton course. Your Personal Workbook will provide most of the content and management information you will need, providing your instructor more time to give students individual attention. There will be just one large-group demonstration throughout the entire course, and very little time will be spent organizing routine class "chores." Nearly all the instructor's time will be available to facilitate your learning on an individual basis.

Your instructor has the teaching experience and expertise to make the PSIS work as well as it was designed. The PSIS system allows the instructor to provide the maximum use of his or her expertise by *facilitating* the learning process for you.

SKILL AND KNOWLEDGE COURSE MODULES

Your PSIS badminton course contains a number of learning activities divided into a series of modules. There are two types of modules: **performance skill** and **badminton knowledge**. Performance skill modules focus on the major psychomotor performance patterns needed to play badminton. The badminton knowledge module contains information on basic game rules and badminton etiquette.

PSIS COURSE MANAGEMENT AND POLICIES

In this section you will learn some of the ways in which the PSIS approach can give you increased control over your own learning. Some course management and policies will come from your Personal Workbook. Others will be communicated to you by your instructor. Be sure that you are familiar with all course management routines and policies.

1. **Dressing for class.** You will need to have proper clothing and footwear in order to participate comfortably and safely in your badminton class. We suggest that you wear lightweight, loose-fitting clothes that will not restrict your range of motion (shorts, T-shirts, and the like). General-purpose court shoes or "cross training" shoes with white soles are recommended. Do not wear running shoes or shoes that will make marks on the floor. Specialized clothing and badminton shoes are not necessary. Be sure to ask your instructor about his or her policies regarding dressing for class.
2. **Equipment.** Your instructor will provide you with all the necessary equipment for class, and with the routines for distributing and collecting equipment each day.
3. **Depositing and distributing Personal Workbooks.** Your instructor will advise you on his or her policy regarding your workbook each day after class. We suggest that the instructor collect all student workbooks at the end of class and bring them to class the next day. Be sure that you know the exact policy to be used, since you cannot participate fully in class without your own workbook.
4. **Practice partners.** Some learning tasks call for you to practice with one or more partners and be checked off by them. Any classmate can be your partner for most tasks. A few tasks will specify that all students in a drill be at the same place in the course learning sequence.
5. **Arriving to class.** Your instructor will inform you about specific routines for arriving to class and beginning each day. Generally, you should (1) arrive at or before the class starting time, (2) locate your own Personal Workbook, (3) complete your stretching and warm-up routine, (4) find a practice partner (if needed at that time), and (5) begin to practice the appropriate learning task. Note that you can begin as soon as you arrive. Except for the first day of instruction, the instructor will not wait to begin the class with all students together. *Arriving before class will allow you extra time to practice your badminton skills.*
6. **Self-checks, partner checks, and instructor checks.** Each learning task in PSIS badminton requires that your mastery be documented (checked

off). Some tasks can be checked off by you, some must be checked off by a partner, and some by your instructor. Items are checked off by the appropriate person initialing and dating the designated area after each checked task in your Personal Workbook. Instructor-checked tasks will require that you practice for a period of time prior to attempting mastery and being checked off. When you are ready, indicated by a series of successful trial blocks, signal the instructor and ask him or her to observe you. If you do not reach the stated criterion, you can return for more practice and signal for the instructor again at a later time. *There is no penalty for not making a mastery criterion. You can try as many times as it takes to be successful.* You may find it helpful to alert the instructor at the beginning of a class in which you anticipate needing his or her observation and checking. The instructor will then be on the lookout for your signal.

7. **Grading.** Your course instructor will inform you about the grading system and related policies to be used in your PSIS badminton class. Be sure you are aware of the specific requirements and procedures for determining your grade.

USING YOUR TIME EFFECTIVELY

Your PSIS badminton course is made up of a series of predetermined learning tasks grouped into eight modules. Your course will have a set number of class days with a set class length. It is important for you to know your own learning pace and to make steady progress toward completing all course requirements. Therefore, you will need to learn how to best use your time in class and to accurately project completion of PSIS badminton before the end of the term. Here are some helpful tips for managing your time.

1. Arrive to class early and begin right away. No signal will be given by the instructor for class to begin.
2. Stay for the entire class period. Do not get into a habit of leaving early.
3. Learn the PSIS course management system right away. The quicker you understand how it works, the sooner you can start using it to your advantage.
4. Do not hesitate to ask the instructor for assistance. Learn and use the class help signal to get the instructor's attention.
5. If there is not enough time to complete a new task in a class, at least *start* it. This will save time the next day.
6. When you are close to finishing a task at the end of a class, try to stay a few minutes late to complete it. This avoids repetitious setup time the next day and the possible loss of your learning momentum.

7. When a practice partner is needed, pair up with the first person you can find, rather than waiting for a certain person. (This is good way to get to know more of your classmates!)
8. Alert the instructor prior to instructor-checked criterion tasks so that he or she will be available when you need observation and a check-off.

PSIS BADMINTON LEARNING MODULES

This section will describe how the PSIS course learning modules are designed. It is important that you know how the PSIS works so that you can take advantage of its individualized learning features. The course learning content is included in two kinds of learning modules: **performance skill** and **badminton knowledge**.

Each *performance skill* module will include the following:

1. A written **introduction** to the skill
2. An **instructor demonstration** of the proper skill techniques
3. Text and photographs that explain the **components** or **phases** of each skill
4. Photographs that highlight the key **performance cues** (these same cues will be presented by the instructor in his or her demonstration).
5. Simple **comprehension tasks** and **readiness drills** to develop initial skill patterns
6. An **error analysis** and **correction section** for self-analyzing common mistakes
7. **Learning tips** for increased proficiency
8. A series of several **criterion tasks** for practicing and demonstrating your skill mastery
9. One or more **challenge tasks** for developing tactical applications of skills in modified competitive situations
10. A **Personal Recording Form** for selected tasks, used to record successful practice trials

The *badminton knowledge* module includes the following:

1. A **reading** on the basic rules of badminton and badminton game strategy
2. A **knowledge quiz** to test your understanding of the rules and strategy

CHARTING YOUR PROGRESS

The last page of your PSIS badminton workbook includes your **Personal Progress Chart**. Your instructor will show you how to correctly label the chart, and the rest is very simple. At the end of each week in the course, put an x above that date, and across from the last task you completed. As the weeks go by, you will begin to see how your individual learning pace projects your successful completion of all course learning tasks.

This introductory section, combined with additional information from your instructor, will allow you to use the PSIS badminton workbook to your full advantage and to learning badminton at your own pace, with highly individualized attention from your instructor. Because PSIS badminton is a complete system for learning the game, it might take you a little time to become familiar with this approach. However, remember that your instructor is there to help when you have questions about the system and when you need individual attention for learning. Now that you know about the PSIS badminton system, you are probably anxious to get started. I hope you enjoy learning badminton with the PSIS approach and that you will become an avid player of this lifelong game. READY...SET...GO!!

MODULE 1

STRETCHING FOR BADMINTON

INTRODUCTION

Flexibility refers to the ability of the muscles, tendons, and ligaments around a joint to move, while providing support and allowing the joint to move smoothly through its entire range-of-motion. Increased flexibility means more supple muscles, which reduces the risk of injury to the muscle when the limb is moved suddenly. The static method is the most commonly recommended stretching technique. It has been shown to be extremely effective in increasing range of motion and, when done slowly and carefully, presents little chance of injury to the muscles.

Some sports and forms of exercise lead to improved flexibility of the involved body part. Badminton, for example, tends to limber the shoulder joint and lower back. Gymnastics can only be accomplished with a high degree of flexibility in virtually all points of the body. Activities such as walking and jogging do not require a large range of motion and do not increase flexibility. This is why it is important that stretching should precede these types of exercises. Stretching not only enhances performance, but it also reduces the risk of injury.

Flexibility should be included during the warm-up phase of an exercise program. This permits for gentle stretching of muscles around the joint before vigorous movement and leads to a slower cool-down, thereby maintaining local blood flow and reducing postexercise soreness.

Although muscular soreness can have many origins, one major cause appears to be damage to the connective tissue elements in the muscles and tendons. No one method of overcoming soreness is available, but adequate stretching appears to aid not only in preventing soreness, but also in relieving it when it already exists.

PERFORMANCE CUES

1. **Warm-up.** Protect the muscle by beginning with a low- to moderate-intensity warm-up for 2 to 3 minutes prior to performing strenuous stretching exercises. Running in place should provide an excellent warm-up.
2. **Do not bounce.** Move into the stretching position slowly, continuing until mild tension is felt. Utilize a static or very slow stretch and hold the position. A ballistic or bouncing stretch can be counterproductive and even cause injury.
3. **Hold the stretch.** The stretch position should be held for a predetermined amount of time. It is suggested that the initial holding position be between 15 and 20 seconds and be gradually increased over the following weeks. As flexibility improves, attempt to hold the stretch slightly longer. When the stretching exercise is complete, the body should be released slowly from the stretch position.
4. **Target zone.** You should not feel pain when stretching a muscle. There is a stretching target zone where *there is tension in the muscle without pain*. It is important to be aware of your own target zone. Stretching at a level below the target zone will not lead to increased flexibility, whereas stretching above this zone will increase the risk of injury.
5. **Breathing.** Do not hold your breath while stretching. Breathing should be slow, rhythmical, and continuous.
6. **Stretch before and after exercise.** Stretching before vigorous exercise prepares the muscles and joints for activity and reduces the risk of injury. Stretching after vigorous exercise is needed to further stretch the muscles. Both warm-up and cool-down are needed.

INSTRUCTOR DEMONSTRATION

Your course instructor will demonstrate each recommended stretching exercise for badminton. Observe the demonstration carefully, making note of the performance cues for each exercise.

Shoulder Stretch (triceps). Elevate one elbow and position the racquet down the middle of your back. Reach behind your back with the other hand and grab the racquet slightly above belt-high. Gently apply force by moving the nonracquet hand down, causing your other elbow to rise (and stretch). Hold the stretch in the target zone for 15 to 20 seconds and slowly release. Repeat this exercise 5 to 8 times with both shoulders. Refer to Photo 1.1.

Photo 1.1
Shoulder stretch

Photo 1.2
Lateral shoulder stretch

Photo 1.3
Lower back and hamstrings
stretch

Lateral Shoulder Stretch. Elevate the arms and grip the racquet at each end. Gently pull down with one arm, stretching the opposite shoulder. Bend your hips in the direction of the pull. Knees should be slightly flexed during the exercise. Hold the stretch in the target zone for 15 to 20 seconds and slowly release. Repeat this exercise 5 to 8 times on both sides of the body. Refer to Photo 1.2.

Lower Back and Hamstrings Stretch. From a standing position and holding the racquet at each end, bend forward at the hips and allow the head and arms to hang downward. Have both knees slightly flexed during this exercise. Hold the stretch in the target zone for 15 to 20 seconds and slowly release. Repeat this exercise 5 to 8 times. Refer to Photo 1.3.

Photo 1.4
Lower Back and Hip extensor stretch

Photo 1.5
Wall stretch

Lower Back and Hip Extensor Stretch. From a supine position, elevate one leg toward your chest. Apply pressure for the stretch with both arms pulling toward the chest. Hold the stretch in the target zone for 15 to 20 seconds and slowly release. Repeat this exercise 5 to 8 times with each leg. Refer to Photo 1.4.

Wall Stretch (gastrocnemius). Take a position 2 to 3 feet from a wall or solid structure. Lean forward and support your body weight with your forearms. Flex one leg and position the other leg to the rear with the front foot flat on the floor. Force your hips forward while keeping the back leg straight. Hold the stretch in the target zone for 15 to 20 seconds and slowly release. Repeat this exercise 5 to 8 times with each leg. Photo 1.5.

COMPREHENSION TASK

Partner-Checked

Pair up with another person in the class. In turn, perform each stretch, while the other observes for proper technique. Have your partner check and initial below when you have performed the stretch just as your instructor demonstrated. If you have questions or need assistance, use the help signal to alert your instructor.

1. Shoulder stretch
2. Lateral shoulder stretch
3. Lower back and hamstrings stretch
4. Lower back and hip extensor stretch
5. Wall stretch

Partner's initials _____   Date completed _____

MODULE 2

BADMINTON BASICS

EQUIPMENT

Badminton requires little equipment to play, one of the reasons for its popularity in so many countries. Badminton equipment is relatively inexpensive and durable. The basic design of the two most essential pieces of equipment, the racquet and the shuttle, has changed little in several decades. The few changes that have occurred are in the materials used for these items.

BADMINTON RACQUET

The striking implement, or racquet, used to play badminton is lightweight and thin. The body of the racquet is made of a metal alloy, and the strings are made of thin nylon cord. The handle grip is commonly wrapped with a thin layer of leather. The standard badminton racquet is shown in Photo 2.1.

Photo 2.1
Badminton racquet

SHUTTLE

The object used in badminton is called the shuttle (not the "birdie"). The shuttle has evolved in many ways since the determination of formal game rules in England in the last decades of the 1800s. Today it comes in two versions, one made with goose feathers and one with nylon "feathers." Feather shuttles are more expensive and far less durable, so their use is typically limited to sanctioned competitions among elite players. Shuttles are made in three different weights, which result in varying flight distances. These differences are not important for beginning players, but as your skills improve you may come to prefer one weight more than the others.

SHOES AND ATTIRE

It is important that you have the proper shoes for playing badminton, to increase comfort and safety. It is not important at this time to have shoes designed specifically for badminton. Shoes rated for general indoor court use or cross training will work well. *Running shoes are not recommended for badminton, because of their narrow soles and limited ankle support.* Finally, make sure your shoes have white soles, not black, so that they will not make marks on the badminton court. Your attire for badminton should include socks, shorts, and a lightweight short-sleeved shirt. Your shorts and shirt should permit a comfortable, full range of motion and provide good ventilation. Badminton is a very active game, and your clothing should allow your body to breathe easily to evaporate perspiration.

COURT AND NET

COURT LAYOUT

It is important that badminton players know the layout of the court. This layout not only defines boundaries for serves and other shots, but it also is used to describe court positioning and shot placement. Illustration 2.1 shows a diagram for the badminton court and the various lines and boundaries. The left side shows the lines for singles play; the right side shows the lines for doubles play. Note that the service return boxes and court boundaries differ for singles and doubles play.

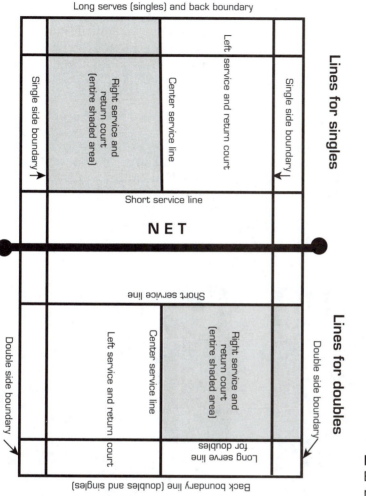

Illustration 2.1
Badminton court and markings

COMPREHENSION TASK

Study Illustration 2.1 until you can identify all the labeled lines on the diagram. Then find a partner and have her or him call out the names of the various parts of the badminton court. After each part is called, walk onto the court and either stand on or point to that part. (*Note:* Because there are so many lines on a relatively small court, do not stand off the court to point.) Repeat this task until you correctly identify every line or area with no mistakes.

NET

The net should be a height of 5 feet 1 inch at either end and 5 feet at the center. It should be held by two posts, secured just outside of the doubles side boundaries. The net should be 2 feet from its top to its bottom, with no vision obstructions.

BADMINTON FUNDAMENTALS

Badminton is a game is which the "little things" count. These include several fundamentals that all beginning players should know and use at all times. The most basic skill in badminton is the **ready position**, which allows the player to move in every direction on the court quickly and equally well. During competition you will not know where your opponent's shot will go until it leaves her or his racquet, so it is important to be in a good ready position to move quickly in all directions. Refer to Photos 2.2A and 2.2B as you read the performance cues for the ready position.

Photo 2.2A
Ready position, front view

Photo 2.2B
Ready position, side view

READY POSITION

1. Your feet should be slightly more than shoulder-width apart, with both feet turned slightly outward.
2. Your knees should bend slightly. Do not lock them into one position.
3. Bend forward at the waist until your heels start to come off the floor, giving you a *floating* weight distribution.
4. Position the racquet in front of you, with the handle at waist height. Do not favor the forehand or backhand sides with your racquet position.

BASICS OF BADMINTON SHOT MAKING

Because the badminton court is small and the shuttle can travel at high speed, it is important to be able to make quick decisions for shot selection and aiming. All basic badminton shots include nine components: (1) court position, (2) aiming area, (3) grip, (4) footwork, (5) contact point, (6) wrist action, (7) trajectory, (8) speed and power, and (9) follow-through. Each component will be discussed in general and later applied specifically to each basic badminton shots.

COURT POSITIONING AND AIMING AREAS

Your position on the court as you prepare to make a shot is an important factor in shot selection. Certain court positions often dictate the kind of shot you can make and where your shot should be aimed. Illustration 2.2 shows the basic court positions for making shots, while Illustration 2.3 indicates the most common aiming areas on your opponent's side of the net. Note that the midcourt area is the optimal area for making shots, but you should not aim your shots to your opponent's midcourt area.

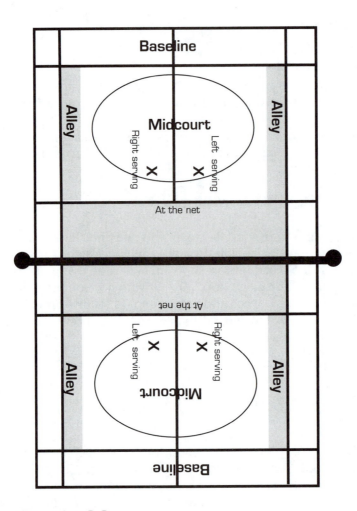

Illustration 2.2
Shot-making areas

COURT POSITIONS FOR MAKING SHOTS

1. Service (right and left)
2. At the net
3. Midcourt
4. Baseline
5. Alleys

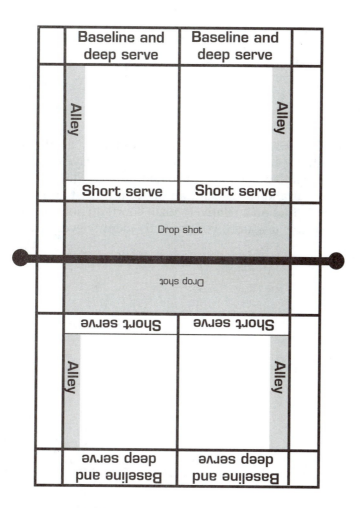

Illustration 2.3
Aiming areas

AIMING AREAS

1. Short serve (serve only)
2. Deep serve (serve only)
3. Drop
4. Alleys
5. Baseline

COMPREHENSION TASK

Study Illustrations 2.2 and 2.3 until you can identify all the labeled court positions and aiming areas. Then find a partner and have him or her call out the names of the various places on the badminton court. After each is called, walk onto the court and either stand in or point to that area. (*Note:* Because there are so many lines on a relatively small court, do not stand off the court to point.) Repeat this task until you correctly identify every area.

GRIPS

Three basic grips are used in badminton. One grip is used for **forehand** shots and one used for **backhand** shots. The **underhand** grip is used for short low serves and some drop shots. Refer to Photos 2.3 through 2.5 as you read the performance cues for each type of grip.

Forehand Grip

1. Hold the shaft of the racquet in your nonstriking hand, with the head of the racquet tilted **upward at a 45-degree angle**, and the rim of the racquet **perpendicular to the floor**.
2. Extend your nonstriking arm to near-full length, with the handle of the racquet **slightly above your waist**.
3. Reach your striking hand out to grasp the racquet handle as if you were **shaking hands** with the handle. The small flat part of the handle should be in the **middle** of the bottom knuckles of your thumb and index finger.
4. Your hand should be on the bottom of the handle, but not overhanging.

Photo 2.3
Forehand grip

Photo 2.4
Backhand grip

Photo 2.5
Underhand grip

5. Comfortably wrap your fingers around the handle, with your index finger slightly separated from your middle finger. This is called a **trigger finger** and gives you added stability and power on your forehand shots.

Backhand grip

1. Hold the shaft of the racquet in your nonstriking hand, with the head of the racquet tilted **upward at a 45-degree angle**, and the rim of the racquet **perpendicular to the floor.**
2. Extend your non-striking arm to near-full length, with the handle of the racquet **slightly above your waist.**
3. Reach your striking hand out to grasp the racquet handle as if you were **shaking hands** with the handle. Rotate the racquet so that the small, flat part of the handle is almost under the bottom knuckle of your index finger. *Key point: Turn the racquet, not your hand.*
4. Your hand should be on the bottom of the handle, but not overhanging.
5. A trigger finger is optional on this grip, but it is a good habit to use one all the time.
6. Place your thumb on the larger flat part of the handle for added stability and power.

Underhand Grip

1. This is an optional grip used for making short low serves and some drop shots.
2. Hold the racquet in front of you with your nonstriking hand on the shaft of the racquet. The racquet face should be parallel to the floor.
3. Place the handle in your striking hand with your palm facing upward.
4. Gently wrap your thumb on the racquet, as if you were holding the handle of a cooking killet.

FOOTWORK

You can use the face of a clock to visualize the proper footwork for the ready position, forehand, and backhand shots. Illustration 2.4 shows foot placement for the ready position. The left foot is at 9 o'clock and the right foot is at 3 o'clock (as if you were looking directly down from above the player). Illustration 2.5 shows foot placement for forehand shots (right-handed players). In the correct position for forehand shots, the right (back) foot is between 4 and 5 o'clock and the left (front) foot is at 1 o'clock. Illustration 2.6 shows foot placement for backhand shots (right-handed players). In the correct position for backhand shots, the left (back) foot is between 7 and 8 o'clock and the left (front) foot is at 11 o'clock.

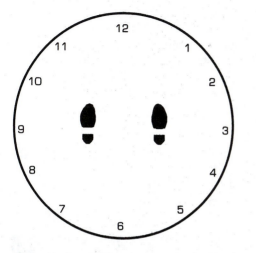

Illustration 2.4
Ready position footwork

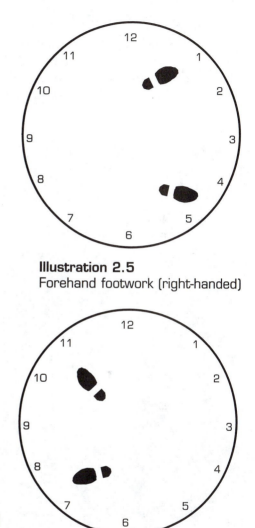

Illustration 2.5
Forehand footwork (right-handed)

Illustration 2.6
Backhand footwork (right-handed)

COMPREHENSION TASK

Select a partner and demonstrate to her or him the ready position with all the correct performance cues. While in the correct ready position, have your partner randomly call out "forehand" or "backhand." You should **quickly** execute the correct footwork and grip for the designated shot. Hold your position and have your partner check for correct execution. Be sure to return to the ready position before the next call is made. Do this 10 times and then switch roles with your partner.

CONTACT POINT

The height of the racquet head at the point of contact largely determines the kind of shot to be made and the trajectory of the shuttle as it travels to your opponent's court. Again, we can use the face of a clock to describe the various points of contact for basic shot making. Refer to Photos 2.6 through 2.9.

Photo 2.6
Clear: 11 to 12 o'clock, moving upward

Photo 2.7
Smash: 1 to 2 o'clock, moving downward

Photo 2.8
Drive: 3 o'clock, horizontal, moving forward

Photo 2.9
Drop: between 3 and 4 o'clock, vertical, moving upward

WRIST ACTION

Each type of shot requires a certain kind of wrist action to determine the correct trajectory and speed. Three types of wrist action are used for basic shot making. Refer to Photos 2.10 through 2.12 as you read each description.

A **firm** wrist has little or no hyperextension (before) and flexion (after) on the shot. This technique is used for shots that require a soft touch on the shuttle when attempting precise accuracy.

Moderate wrist action has some hyperextension (before) and some flexion (after) on the shot. It is used for medium-ranged shots with medium trajectory when accuracy is not critical.

Full wrist action has complete hyperextension (before) and full flexion (after) on the shot. It provides maximum power, speed, and trajectory when needed. With this wrist action, accuracy is reduced in favor of increased power and speed.

Photo 2.10
Firm wrist

Photo 2.11
Moderate wrist action

Photo 2.12
Full wrist action

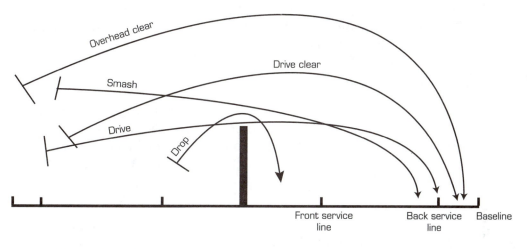

Illustration 2.7
Shot trajectories

TRAJECTORY

Each kind of badminton shot calls for a certain trajectory as the shuttle travels to your opponent's court. The trajectory often determines whether your opponent can return with an offensive or defensive shot back to your side. In general, the higher the trajectory that you attempt, the deeper into your opponent's court you should aim (see Illustration 2.7).

- A **low** trajectory is used for drop shots that fall close to the net on your opponent's side.
- A **downward** trajectory is used for smash shots.
- A **medium** trajectory is used for drive shots that fall in the middle and back of your opponent's court.
- A **high** trajectory is used for clear shots that fall deep in your opponent's court.

POWER AND SPEED

Power and speed are directly related in badminton. The more power you use on a shot, the faster the shuttle travels coming off your racquet. The exact time it takes for the shuttle to reach your aiming area is determined by the trajectory you choose. For this book, power will is described at three levels: **low** (slow, with short travel), **medium** (moderate speed and distance), and **full** (high speed, used at any distance).

FOLLOW THROUGH

A badminton shot is not complete at the moment of contact with the shuttle. Correct execution includes the proper follow-through needed for each type of shot. The follow-through consists of a combination of arm motion and wrist action. In general, the length of the follow- through determines the wrist action. Refer to Photos 2.13 through 2.15.

SHOT MAKING FUNDAMENTALS

It is important that you have a basic repertoire of shots as a beginning player. Develop and improve these shots until you are ready for more advanced shots and placements. This book will familiarize you with several basic badminton shots, develop your skills in hitting them, and help you to recognize when and how to use each shot. Before you begin this section of the course, it is important to learn a few fundamentals about shot making in badminton.

Every shot you make on the court should have one of two strategic purposes. It should be either an attacking (offensive) shot or a defensive shot. The strategic purpose of an attacking shot is to prevent your opponent from making any return so that you can win the rally on that shot. The strategic purpose of a defensive shot is to prevent your opponent from making his or her own attacking shot in return. This purpose can be achieved in two ways: (1) by forcing him/her to run far to make the return or (2) by intentionally moving him or her out of the primary attacking zones on the court (usually to the back of the court).

Proper shot selection, trajectory, and placement in your opponent's court are all important in badminton shot making. Therefore, as the shuttle is coming across the net you must quickly decide (1) to hit an attacking or defensive shot, (2) which specific shot you will use, (3) its trajectory, and (4) the best aiming area to achieve your objective. This quick strategic decision making and execution are what make badminton so exciting to play! Your PSIS Personal Workbook will cover the basic shots for beginning-level players, allowing you to play at a proficient level at the end of the course.

Photo 2.13
Short follow-through, firm wrist

Photo 2.14
Medium follow-through, moderate
wrist

Photo 2.15
Full follow-through, full wrist

MODULE 3

SERVING

INTRODUCTION

Every point in a badminton match begins with a serve. It is regarded as the most important shot in the game, since the server holds a brief advantage in using her or his serve to determine the opponent's next shot. This advantage is lost once a rally starts. A full explanation of game rules is provided in Module 8, but in order to practice your serves correctly, you will need to know some of the basic rules for this part of badminton.

BASIC SERVING RULES

1. All serves must be made from the proper serving box, as determined by the game score. The server must be fully in the service box, with no part of either foot touching the boundary until contact with the shuttle is made.
2. The shuttle must be dropped with the nonstriking hand and contacted before it hits the floor.
3. The shuttle must be contacted with the striking hand clearly above the top of the racquet head (Photos 3.1A and B). If the contact point is unclear, it is a fault.
4. The server cannot try to deceive the returner by obscuring the view of the shuttle, faking striking attempts, or serving before the returner is ready.
5. The serve must fall into the service box diagonally across from the box in which it originates. *A shuttle that lands on a service boundary line is considered to be in the box.*
6. A serve that makes contact with the net is a fault and results in the loss of service.

Photo 3.1A
Legal service (hand above racquet)

Photo 3.1B
Illegal service contact (hand below racquet)

STANCE

1. Although the two most often used serves are struck quite differently, it is good strategy to use only one stance for all serves. This prevents your opponent from anticipating which serve you will hit each time. Refer to Photo 3.2.
2. Set up using the forehand footwork: back foot at 5 o'clock and front foot at 1 o'clock.
3. Rotate your hips toward the net so that you are facing directly to the proper service return box.
4. Hold the shuttle in front of you, gripping the feathers with your thumb and forefinger in your nonstriking hand.
5. Drop the shuttle straight down as you take the racquet back.

TYPES OF SERVES

Two kinds of serves are typically used by beginners: the low short serve and the high deep serve. The objective for both serves is to force your opponent

Photo 3.2
Stance for serving

into a **defensive** return shot so that you can return it with an attacking shot. It is good strategy to always serve from the same place in the appropriate service box and to use the same setup for both types of serves. This prevents your opponent detecting which serve is being played and reduces his or her reaction time on the service return.

Three strategies can be used to decide which serve to play against an opponent: (1) use the serve that she or he is least effective in returning, (2) use a random pattern between the two serves to reduce your opponent's anticipation and reaction time; or (3) let your opponent's setup position determine the best serve (if she or he does not set up in the middle of the service return box). This is a very important part of badminton strategy.

LOW SHORT SERVE

The low short serve is used to move your opponent to the front of the service return box, forcing him or her to return with a nonattacking shot: either a drop shot or a clear. This serve is most effective when aimed to your opponent's backhand side.

INSTRUCTOR DEMONSTRATION

Your course instructor will provide you with an explanation and demonstration of the key performance cues for the low short serve. If you have questions, be sure to ask them before proceeding to the individualized task sequence. Refer to Photos 3.3A through C as your instructor explains and demonstrates each of the performance cues for the low short serve.

Photo 3.3A
Backswing for low short serve

Photo 3.3B
Contact point for low short serve

Photo 3.3C
Follow-through for low short serve

PERFORMANCE CUES

1. **Court position:** Near center line, 2 to 3 feet from the short service line
2. **Aiming area:** One to two feet over the opposite short service line, opponent's backhand side preferred
3. **Grip:** Forehand or underhand
4. **Footwork:** Forehand setup
5. **Contact point:** Between 3 and 4 o'clock (vertical, lifting upward)
6. **Wrist action:** Firm
7. **Trajectory:** Low, as close to the net as possible
8. **Power and speed:** Low
9. **Follow through:** Short

COMPREHENSION TASK

Find a partner and demonstrate to each other the proper performance cues for the low short serve *without hitting the shuttle*. Be sure to provide feedback to each other for correct and incorrect performance cues until both of you can execute this shot correctly.

LEARNING TIPS

1. Hold the feather of the shuttle with the thumb and index finger of your nonstriking hand. The tip of the shuttle should point down.
2. Release the shuttle straight down as your racquet is coming forward.
3. With your wrist firm, try to lift the shuttle over the net and into the aiming area.
4. Be sure to complete your follow-through, even this short one.

READINESS DRILL

3-1. From the correct court position in the service area, attempt 40 low short serves from each service side. Do not be concerned with a specific aiming area at this time. Use these shots to gauge the proper contact point, power, and trajectory for the low short serve.

If you experience difficulty with the readiness drill, refer to the **Performance Cues** and review each cue as presented. If you still have difficulty, ask your course instructor to assist you in applying these techniques.

Common Errors and Their Correction

Error	Correction
Error	**Correction**
The serve does not go straight.	1. Make sure your footwork is correct on setup. 2. Make a more vertical swing path.
The serve goes too short or into the net.	1. Use a little more power (but do not add more wrist action). 2. Increase your lifting action.
The serve goes too far.	Reduce power and wrist action (do not move back in the service box).
Inconsistent shots, no set pattern for errors.	1. Recheck all performance cues without striking the shuttle. 2. Continue the readiness drill until you are more consistent.

CRITERION TASKS FOR LOW SHORT SERVES: SELF-CHECKED

Choose a service box and the proper service return box for this task. Mark off a parallel line 3 feet past the opposite short service line. The resulting rectangle is your aiming area for this task (see Illustration 3.1). Set up for your serves in the proper position on one service court. Practice your low short serves in blocks of 10 shots, keeping a record of how many shots in each group of 10 have a low trajectory and land in the aiming area.

1. *Position:* Serving position in appropriate box
2. *Aiming area:* Marked rectangle in opposite service return box
3. *Trajectory:* Low
4. *Shuttle:* Self-tossed, with legal contact
5. *Criterion:* 8 of 10 in aiming area, four sets from both service sides

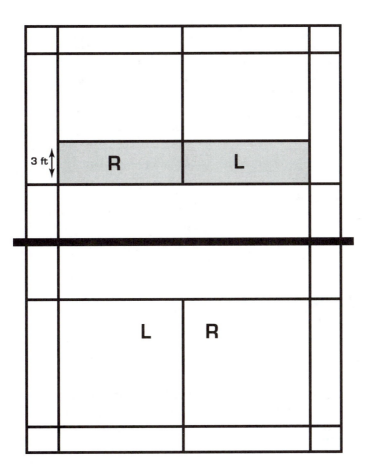

Illustration 3.1
Criterion Task 3-1 and 3-2

CRITERION TASK 3-1

From the Right Service Side

Practice this task in blocks of 10 serves. Record the number of successful low short serves for each block on the **Personal Recording Form.** When four block scores reach or exceed 8 out of 10, initial and date in the space provided.

Personal Recording Form									
Block 1	Block 2	Block 3	Block 4	Block 5	Block 6	Block 7	Block 8	Block 9	Block 10
___/10	___/10	___/10	___/10	___/10	___/10	___/10	___/10	___/10	___/10

Your initials _____   Date completed _____

CRITERION TASK 3-2

From the Left Service Side

Practice this task in blocks of 10 serves. Record the number of successful low short serves for each block on the **Personal Recording Form.** When four individual block scores reach or exceed 8 out of 10, initial and date in the space provided.

Personal Recording Form									
Block 1	Block 2	Block 3	Block 4	Block 5	Block 6	Block 7	Block 8	Block 9	Block 10
___/10	___/10	___/10	___/10	___/10	___/10	___/10	___/10	___/10	___/10

Your initials _____   Date completed _____

Criterion Tasks for Low Short Serves: Partner-Checked

Choose a service box and the opposite service return box for this task. Mark off a parallel line 2 feet beyond the opposite short service line. Next, mark a line from the midpoint of the short service line to the parallel line, making a small rectangle (see Illustration 3.2). **Choose one of the small rectangles on the proper side as your aiming area.** Set up for your serves in the proper position on one service court. Practice your low short serves in blocks of 10 shots, keeping a record of how many shots in each group have a low trajectory and land in the aiming area.

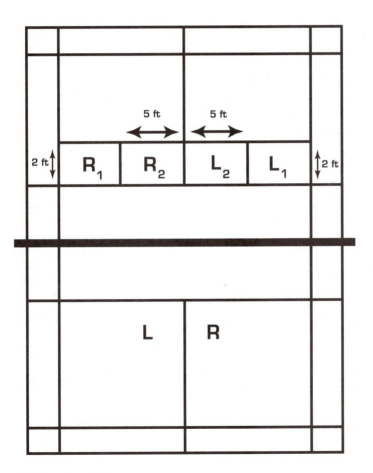

Illustration 3.2
Criterion Task 3-3 and 3-4

1. *Position:* Serving position in appropriate box
2. *Aiming area:* Small rectangle in opposite service return box
3. *Trajectory:* Low
4. *Shuttle:* Self-tossed, with legal contact
5. *Criterion:* 7 of 10 in aiming area, three sets from both service sides

CRITERION TASK 3-3

From the Right Service Side

Practice this task in blocks of 10 serves. Record the number of successful low short serves for each block on the **Personal Recording Form**. When your block scores reach or exceed 7 out of 10, ask your partner to observe and witness your successful completion of three blocks. Once completed, have your partner initial and date in the space provided.

Personal Recording Form									
Block 1	Block 2	Block 3	Block 4	Block 5	Block 6	Block 7	Block 8	Block 9	Block 10
___/10	___/10	___/10	___/10	___/10	___/10	___/10	___/10	___/10	___/10

Partner's initials _____   Date completed _____

CRITERION TASK 3-4

From the Left Service Side

Practice this task in blocks of 10 serves. Record the number of successful low short serves for each block on the Personal Recording Form. When your block scores reach or exceed 7 out of 10, ask your partner to observe and witness your successful completion of three blocks. Once completed, have your partner initial and date in the space provided.

Personal Recording Form									
Block 1	Block 2	Block 3	Block 4	Block 5	Block 6	Block 7	Block 8	Block 9	Block 10
___/10	___/10	___/10	___/10	___/10	___/10	___/10	___/10	___/10	___/10

Partner's initials _____   Date completed _____

HIGH DEEP SERVE

INTRODUCTION

As the name indicates, the high deep serve is used with a trajectory high enough to get over your opponent's outstretched arm and racquet and deep enough to force your opponent to move to the back of his or her court to make the return. Most often this is a defensive serve, used to set up your next shot, anticipating a weak return from your opponent. This serve is most effective when aimed to your opponent's backhand side.

INSTRUCTOR DEMONSTRATION

Your course instructor will provide you with an explanation and demonstration of the key performance cues for the high deep serve. If you have questions, be sure to ask them before proceeding to the individualized task sequence. Refer to Photos 3.4A through C as your instructor explains and demonstrates each performance cue for the high deep serve.

Photo 3.4A
Backswing for high deep serve

Photo 3.4B
Contact point for high deep serve

Photo 3.4C
Follow-through for high deep serve

PERFORMANCE CUES

1. *Court position:* Near center line, 2 to 3 feet from the short service line
2. *Aiming area:* Singles: between the long service line for doubles and the back boundary line; backhand side preferred. Doubles: less than 2 feet inside the doubles' long service line; backhand side preferred
3. *Grip:* Forehand
4. *Footwork:* Forehand setup
5. *Contact point:* Between 3 and 4 o'clock (vertical, moving upward)
6. *Wrist action:* Full, with hard upward extension
7. *Trajectory:* High, over the top of your opponent's outstretched racquet
8. *Speed and power:* Full
9. *Follow through:* Full

COMPREHENSION TASK

Find a partner and demonstrate to each other the proper performance cues for the high deep serve without *hitting the shuttle*. Be sure to provide feedback to each other for correct and incorrect performance cues until both of you can execute this shot correctly.

LEARNING TIPS

1. Hold the feather of the shuttle with the thumb and index finger of your nonstriking hand. The tip of the shuttle should point down.
2. Release the shuttle straight down as your racquet is coming forward.
3. Use an upward, full wrist action to hit the shuttle high and deep into the aiming area.
4. Be sure to complete your follow-through.

READINESS DRILL

3.2   From the correct court position in the service area, attempt 40 high deep serves from each service side. Do not be concerned with a specific aiming area at this time. Use these shots to gauge the proper contact point, power, and trajectory for the serve.

If you experience difficulty with the readiness drill, refer to the **Performance Cues** and review each cue as presented. If you still have difficulty, ask your course instructor to assist you in applying these techniques.

Common Errors and Their Correction

Error	Correction
The serve does not go straight.	1. Make sure your footwork is correct on setup. 2. Make a more vertical swing path.
The serve goes too long.	1. Use a little more power and wrist action. 2. Increase your lifting action.
Inconsistent shots, no set pattern for errors.	1. Recheck all performance cues without striking the shuttle. 2. Continue the readiness drill until you are more consistent.

Criterion Tasks for High Deep Serves: Self-Checked

Choose one service box and the proper service return box for this task. Mark off a line 8 feet from the back boundary of the opposite service return box. The resulting rectangle is your aiming area for this task (see Illustration 3.3). Set up for your serves in the proper position in the service court. Practice your high deep serves in blocks of 10 shots, keeping a record of how many shots in each group have a high trajectory and land in the aiming area.

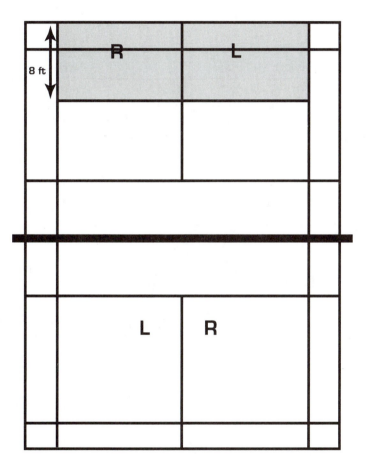

Illustration 3.3
Criterion Task 3-5 and 3-6

1. *Position:* Serving position in appropriate box
2. *Aiming area:* Marked rectangle in opposite service return box
3. *Trajectory:* High
4. *Shuttle:* Self-tossed, with legal contact
5. *Criterion:* 8 of 10 in aiming area, four sets from both service sides

CRITERION TASK 3-5

From the Right Service Side

Practice this task in blocks of 10 serves. Record the number of successful high deep serves for each block on the **Personal Recording Form.** When four block scores reach or exceed 8 out of 10, initial and date in the space provided.

Personal Recording Form									
Block 1	Block 2	Block 3	Block 4	Block 5	Block 6	Block 7	Block 8	Block 9	Block 10
__/10	__/10	__/10	__/10	__/10	__/10	__/10	__/10	__/10	__/10

Your initials _____   Date completed _____

CRITERION TASK 3-6

From the Left Service Side

Practice this task in blocks of 10 serves. Record the number of successful high deep serves for each block on the **Personal Recording Form**. When four blockscores reach or exceed 8 out of 10, initial and date in the space provided.

Personal Recording Form									
Block 1	Block 2	Block 3	Block 4	Block 5	Block 6	Block 7	Block 8	Block 9	Block 10
__/10	__/10	__/10	__/10	__/10	__/10	__/10	__/10	__/10	__/10

Your initials _____   Date completed _____

Criterion Tasks for High Deep Serve: Partner-Checked

Choose one service box and the proper service return box for this task. Your aiming area is the rectangle formed by the singles side boundary, the center service line, the back boundary, and the doubles back service line (see Illustration 3.4). Have a partner stand in the center of the opposite service return box with his or her arm stretched and racquet reaching overhead. Set up for your serves in the proper position in the service court.

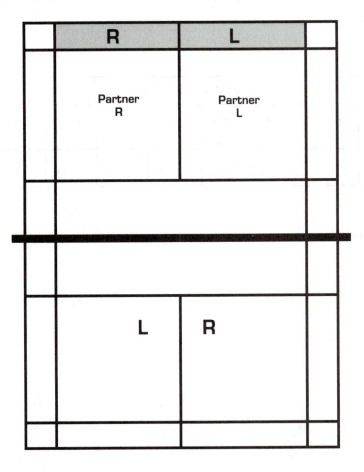

Illustration 3.4
Criterion Task 3-7 and 3-8

1. *Position:* Serving position in appropriate box
2. *Aiming area:* Marked rectangle in opposite service return box
3. *Trajectory:* Over your partner's outstretched arm and racquet
4. *Shuttle:* Self-tossed, with legal contact
5. *Criterion:* 6 of 10, three sets from both service sides

CRITERION TASK 3-7

From the Right Service Side

Practice this task in blocks of 10 serves. A successful serve is one that goes over your partner's outstretched arm and racquet and lands in the legal serving box. Record the number of successful high deep serves for each block on the **Personal Recording Form.** When your block scores reach or exceed 6 out of 10, ask your partner to observe and witness your successful completion of three blocks. Once completed, have your partner initial and date in the space provided.

Personal Recording Form									
Block 1	Block 2	Block 3	Block 4	Block 5	Block 6	Block 7	Block 8	Block 9	Block 10
__/10	__/10	__/10	__/10	__/10	__/10	__/10	__/10	__/10	__/10

Partner's initials _____   Date completed _____

CRITERION TASK 3-8

From the Left Service Side

Practice this task in blocks of 10 serves. A successful serve is one that goes over your partner's outstretched arm and racquet and lands in the legal serving box. Record the number of successful high deep serves for each block on the **Personal Recording Form.** When your block scores reach or exceed 6 out of 10, ask your partner to observe and witness your successful completion of three blocks. Once completed, have your partner initial and date in the space provided.

Personal Recording Form									
Block 1	Block 2	Block 3	Block 4	Block 5	Block 6	Block 7	Block 8	Block 9	Block 10
___/10	___/10	___/10	___/10	___/10	___/10	___/10	___/10	___/10	___/10

Partner's initials _____   Date completed _____

Criterion Tasks for Serving: Instructor-Checked

Refer to the targeting layout in Illustration 3.5, which includes five aiming areas and their designated points. Note that the targeting is different (mirrored) from the right and left sides, reflecting a right-handed opponent's orientation. Any serve landing outside the legal service return box results in 0 points. Landing in the large area in the middle results in 1 point, because serves to this area can be returned easily with attacking shots. Choose one service box from which to hit your serves, and set up the diagonal service return box according to the layout. Practice serves in blocks of 10 shots, hitting 5 low short serves and 5 high deep serves in each block. *Subtract 1 point from any serve that lands in a scoring area, but does not have the proper trajectory*. Example, a 3-point deep serve is reduced to 2 points due to a low trajectory.

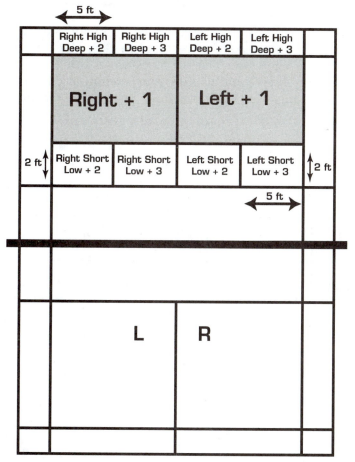

Illustration 3.5
Criterion Task 3-9 and 3-10

1. *Position:* Serving position in appropriate box
2. *Aiming area:* As designated for each type of serve.
3. *Trajectory:* Correct for each type of serve attempted.
4. *Shuttle:* Self-tossed, with legal contact
5. *Criterion:* Score 16 or more points on one block from each side (30 points maximum)

CRITERION TASK 3-9

From the Right Service Side

Practice this task in blocks of 10 serves (5 low short and 5 high deep, in any order). Record the number of points scored in each block on the **Personal Recording Form.** When your practice block scores reach or exceed 20, ask your instructor to observe and witness your attempt at criterion. Once you have scored 16 or higher in one block, have your instructor initial and date in the space provided.

Personal Recording Form									
Block 1	Block 2	Block 3	Block 4	Block 5	Block 6	Block 7	Block 8	Block 9	Block 10
___/10	___/10	___/10	___/10	___/10	___/10	___/10	___/10	___/10	___/10

Instructor's initials _____   Date completed _____

CRITERION TASK 3-10

From the Left Service Side

Practice this task in blocks of 10 serves (5 low short and 5 high deep, in any order). Record the number of points scored in each block on the **Personal Recording Form**. When your block scores reach or exceed 16, ask your instructor to observe and witness your attempt at criterion. Once you have scored 16 or higher in one block, have your instructor initial and date in the space provided.

Personal Recording Form									
Block 1	Block 2	Block 3	Block 4	Block 5	Block 6	Block 7	Block 8	Block 9	Block 10
___/10	___/10	___/10	___/10	___/10	___/10	___/10	___/10	___/10	___/10

Instructor's initials _____   Date completed _____

CHALLENGE TASK FOR SERVING

Find one or more classmates who have also completed the serving module and have been checked off by the instructor on the previous task. Set up a court in the same way as the last task, and use the same scoring system. Start serving from the right service box, aiming for the appropriate box on the other court. Taking turns, each player will make one serve and record the proper number of points on each serve. Each player will get 10 serves (5 low short ones and 5 high deep, in any order). The player with the most points out of 10 serves wins the challenge. Repeat the challenge from the left side. There is no criterion for this task. Repeat the challenge as many times as you wish and with several classmates before moving on to the next module.

MODULE 4

CLEARS

INTRODUCTION

Clears are usually defensive shots used to move your opponent to the back of the court to prevent an attacking shot in return. Clears should have a high trajectory and land within 4 feet of the opposite back boundary. Clears can be hit with the overhead technique or the drive technique from either the forehand or backhand side. Clears can be made from any part of your court, but should always be aimed for the back area of your opponent's court with a high trajectory. It is a good strategy to hit your clears to your opponent's backhand side whenever possible.

FOREHAND DRIVE CLEAR

The forehand drive technique is used to hit a clear when the shuttle comes to you on a medium trajectory. Your objective is to return the shuttle high and deep, forcing your opponent into the extreme back part of the court, preferably on his or her backhand side. *Once you hit a clear, it is good strategy to move to the center of your own court in anticipation of your opponent's return.*

INSTRUCTOR DEMONSTRATION

Your course instructor will provide you with an explanation and demonstration of the key performance cues for the forehand drive clear. If you have questions, be sure to ask them before proceeding to the individualized task sequence. Refer to Photos 4.1A through C as your instructor explains and demonstrates each of the performance cues for the forehand drive clear.

Photo 4.1A
Backswing for forehand drive clear

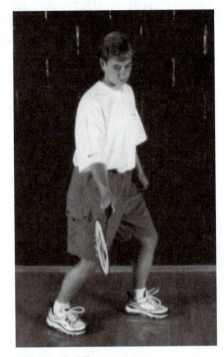

Photo 4.1B
Contact point for forehand drive clear

Photo 4.1C
Follow-through for forehand drive clear

PERFORMANCE CUES

1. **Court position:** Anywhere, usually from the middle or back
2. **Aiming area:** Within 4 feet of the opposite back boundary, opponent's backhand side preferred
3. **Grip:** Forehand
4. **Footwork:** Forehand
5. **Contact point:** 3 o'clock (horizontal, with slight upward action)
6. **Wrist action:** Full, with slight upward lift
7. **Trajectory:** High
8. **Power and speed:** Full
9. **Follow-through:** Full, to eye level

COMPREHENSION TASK

Find a partner and demonstrate to each other the proper performance cues for the forehand drive clear *without hitting the shuttle.* Be sure to provide feedback to each other for correct and incorrect performance cues until both of you can execute this shot correctly.

LEARNING TIPS

1. Be sure to step into this shot. Do not try to hit it with your arm and wrist only.
2. Begin this shot from the ready position and be sure to have your back foot firmly planted before you begin your swing. This increases power and accuracy.

READINESS DRILLS

4.1. Stand in the center of your court. Beginning from the ready position, toss the shuttle to yourself on the forehand side and hit a drive clear. Be sure your toss is fully to your side. Do not toss it directly in front of yourself. At the start, do not be concerned with trajectory or accuracy; just begin to develop the proper techniques and consistency. Hit 40 forehand drive clears, or continue this task until you can consistently hit shots with the proper power and trajectory.

4.2. Repeat the first task with a partner by having him or her stand in the center of the opposite court and gently hit shuttles to your forehand side. **Be sure you start from the ready position at the center of your court for all shots.** You will need to move into proper position to make your shots. Again, do not be concerned with power or accuracy at the beginning. Work on moving into position and using the proper techniques with consistency. Hit 40 forehand drive clears, or continue this task until you can consistently hit shots with the proper power and trajectory.

If you experience difficulty with the readiness drill, refer to the **Performance Cues** and review each cue as presented. If you still have difficulty, ask your course instructor to assist you in applying these techniques.

Common Errors and Their Correction

Error	Correction
Not enough power to reach back of opponent's court.	1. Be sure to plant your back foot and step into the shot. 2. Use more power and a full wrist action on the swing.
Low trajectory.	1. Use lifting action with arm and wrist at point of contact. 2. Be sure to. complete the follow through.
Poor contact (no control).	1. Watch your racquet head make contact with the shuttle before you look up. 2. Be sure to move into position . and plant your back foot firmly before you begin your swing.

CRITERION TASK 4-1

Forehand Drive Clear: Partner-Checked

Mark off 3 feet from the baseline of your opponent's court. Place cones or markers at this line (refer to Illustration 4.1). Stand in a good ready position around the middle of your court (X). Your partner will stand in the middle of the opposite court (P) and hit soft shots to your forehand side with a medium trajectory. If an incoming shot is not to your forehand side, do not attempt to return it. Once your partner hits the shot to you, he or she should raise their racquet in the air overhead. Your clears should pass over your partner's raised racquet, indicating proper trajectory.

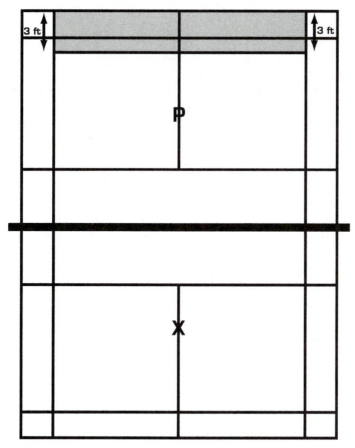

Illustration 4.1
Criterion Task 4-1

1. *Court position:* Middle
2. *Shuttle:* Hit from a partner, standing in middle of the opposite court; your partner's shots should have a medium or high trajectory to you
3. *Trajectory:* Over outstretched racquet of your partner
4. *Aiming area:* Within 3 feet of opposite back boundary
5. *Criterion:* 7 of 10 with proper trajectory and landing in the aiming area, four sets.

   Practice forehand drive clear returns of your partner's shots to the aiming area and with the proper trajectory. *If his or her shot is not to your forehand side or cannot be hit with a clear, do not count it.* Practice this task in blocks of 10 shots. Record the number of successful shots for each block on the **Personal Recording Form**. When your scores reach or exceed 7 out of 10 on four blocks, ask your partner to initial and date in the space provided.

Personal Recording Form									
Block 1	Block 2	Block 3	Block 4	Block 5	Block 6	Block 7	Block 8	Block 9	Block 10
___/10	___/10	___/10	___/10	___/10	___/10	___/10	___/10	___/10	___/10

Partner's initials _____   Date completed _____

BACKHAND DRIVE CLEAR

The backhand drive technique is used to hit a clear when the shuttle comes to you on a medium trajectory. Your objective is to return the shuttle high and deep, forcing your opponent into the extreme back part of the court, preferably on his or her backhand side. *Once you hit a clear, it is good strategy to move to the center of your own court in anticipation of your opponent's return.*

INSTRUCTOR DEMONSTRATION

Your course instructor will provide you with an explanation and demonstration of the key performance cues for the backhand drive clear. If you have questions, be sure to ask them before proceeding to the individualized task sequence. Refer to Photos 4.2A through C as your instructor explains and demonstrates each performance cue for the backhand drive clear.

Photo 4.2A
Backswing for backhand drive clear

Photo 4.2B
Contact position for back-hand drive clear

Photo 4.2C
Follow-through for backhand drive clear

PERFORMANCE CUES

1. **Court position:** Anywhere, usually from middle to back
2. **Aiming area:** Within 4 feet of the opposite back boundary, opponent's backhand side preferred
3. **Grip:** Backhand
4. **Footwork:** Backhand
5. **Contact point:** 9 o'clock (horizontal, with slight upward action)
6. **Wrist action:** Full, with upward lift
7. **Trajectory:** High
8. **Power and speed:** Full
9. **Follow-through:** Full, to eye level

COMPREHENSION TASK

Find a partner and demonstrate to each other the proper performance cues for the backhand drive clear without hitting the shuttle. Be sure to provide feedback to each other for correct and incorrect performance cues until both of you can execute this shot correctly.

LEARNING TIPS

1. Be sure to step into this shot. Do not try to hit it with your arm and wrist only.
2. Be sure to keep your striking arm elbow bent and close to your body. Do not lead with your elbow.
3. Begin this shot from the ready position and be sure to have your back foot firmly planted before you begin your swing. This increases power and accuracy.

READINESS DRILLS

4.3. Stand in the center of your court. Beginning from the ready position, toss the shuttle to yourself on the backhand side and hit a drive clear. Be sure your toss is fully to your side. Do not toss it directly in front of yourself. At the start, do not be concerned with trajectory or accuracy; just begin to develop the proper techniques and consistency. Hit 40 backhand drive clears, or continue this task until you can consistently hit shots with the proper power and trajectory.

4.4. Repeat the first task with a partner by having her or him stand in the center of the opposite court and gently hit shuttles to your backhand side. Be sure you start from the ready position at the center of your court for all shots. You will need to move into proper position to make your shots. Again, do not be concerned with power or accuracy at the beginning. Work on moving into position and using the proper techniques with consistency. Hit 40 backhand drive clears, or continue this task until you can consistently hit shots with the proper power and trajectory.

If you experience difficulty with the readiness drill, refer to the **Performance Cues** and review each cue as presented. If you still have difficulty, ask your course instructor to assist you in applying these techniques.

Common Errors and Their Correction

Error	Correction
Not enough power to reach back of opponent's court.	1. Be sure to plant your back foot and step into the shot. 2. Use more power and a full wrist action on the swing. 3. Keep your elbow close to your body before contact. Leading with your elbow greatly reduces power.
Low trajectory.	1. Use lifting action with arm and wrist at point of contact. 2. Be sure to complete the follow-through. 3. Check contact point (usually too high).
Poor contact (no control).	1. Watch your racquet head make contact with the shuttle before you look up. 2. Be sure to move into position and plant your back foot firmly before you begin your swing.

CRITERION TASK 4-2

Backhand Drive Clear: Partner-Checked

Mark off 4 feet from the baseline of your opponent's court. Place cones or markers at this line (refer to Illustration 4.2). Stand in a good ready position around the middle of your court (X). Your partner will stand in the middle of the opposite court (P) and hit soft shots to your backhand side with a medium or trajectory. If an incoming shot is not to your backhand side, do not attempt to return it. Once your partner hits the shot to you, she or he should raise the racquet in the air overhead. Your clears should pass over your partner's raised racquet, indicating proper trajectory.

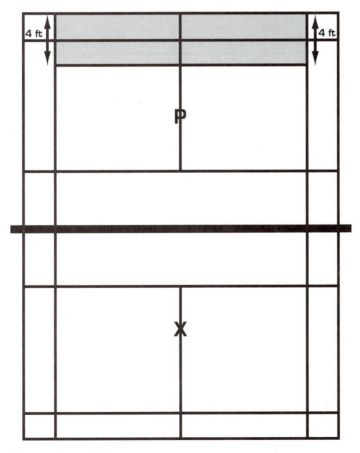

Illustration 4.2
Criterion Task 4-2

1. *Court position:* Middle
2. *Shuttle:* Hit from a partner, standing in center of the opposite court; your partner's shots should have a medium or high trajectory to you
3. *Trajectory:* Over outstretched racquet of your partner
4. *Aiming area:* Within 4 feet of opposite back boundary
5. *Criterion:* 6 of 10 with proper trajectory and landing in the aiming area, three sets

Practice backhand drive clear returns of your partner's shots to the aiming area and with the proper trajectory. *If her or his shot is not to your backhand side or cannot be hit with a clear, do not count it.* Practice this task in blocks of 10 serves. Record the number of successful shots for each block on the **Personal Recording Form**. When your scores reach or exceed 6 out of 10 on three blocks ask your partner to initial and date in the space provided.

Personal Recording Form									
Block 1	Block 2	Block 3	Block 4	Block 5	Block 6	Block 7	Block 8	Block 9	Block 10
__/10	__/10	__/10	__/10	__/10	__/10	__/10	__/10	__/10	__/10

Partner's initials _____   Date completed _____

OVERHEAD CLEAR

The overhead clear is a defensive shot used to return a clear shot made to you. Your position when making an overhead clear is determined by where the shuttle is coming down on your side. If the shuttle is coming down just inside your baseline, you will need to use the overhead clear for your return. If the shuttle is coming down anywhere except near your baseline, you can use a forehand, backhand, or overhead clear. As with any clear shot, you should aim the overhead clear for the back of your opponent's court, preferably to her or his backhand side.

INSTRUCTOR DEMONSTRATION

Your course instructor will provide you with an explanation and demonstration of the key performance cues for the overhead clear. If you have questions, be sure to ask them before proceeding to the individualized task sequence. Refer to Photos 4.3A through C as your instructor explains and demonstrates each performance cue for the overhead clear.

Photo 4.3A
Backswing for overhead clear

Photo 4.3C
Follow-through for overhead clear

Photo 4.3B
Contact point for overhead clear

PERFORMANCE CUES

1. **Court position:** Anywhere, usually from middle to back
2. **Aiming area:** Within 4 feet of the opposite back boundary, opponent's backhand side preferred
3. **Grip:** Forehand
4. **Footwork:** Forehand, with shorter stride
5. **Contact point:** Between 11 and 12 o'clock with upward action
6. **Wrist action:** Full
7. **Trajectory:** High
8. **Power and speed:** Full
9. **Follow-through:** Full, down to waist level

COMPREHENSION TASK

Find a partner and demonstrate to each other the proper performance cues for the overhead clear *without hitting the shuttle.* Be sure to provide feedback to each other for correct and incorrect performance cue, until both of you can execute this shot correctly.

LEARNING TIPS

1. This shot is used only to return an overhead clear from your opponent.
2. Be sure to move to get under the shuttle to make this shot. Line it up as if it were going to land on top of your head.
3. Keep your feet under you for this shot. The step forward is a small one.

READINESS DRILL

4.5. Stand in the center of your court in the ready position. Have your partner hit high deep serves to your forehand side. Move into position and hit overhead clears in return. At the start, do not be concerned with trajectory or accuracy; just begin to develop the proper techniques and consistency. Hit 40 overhead clears, or continue this task until you can consistently hit shots with the proper power and trajectory.

If you experience difficulty with the readiness drill, refer to the **Performance Cues** and review each cue as presented. If you still have difficulty, ask your course instructor to assist you in applying these techniques.

Common Errors and Their Correction

Error	Correction
Not enough power to reach back of opponent's court.	1. Be sure to plant your back foot and step into the shot. 2. Use more power and a full wrist action on the swing.
Low trajectory.	1. Line up the shuttle on your forehead. 2. Be sure to complete the follow through.
Poor contact (no control).	1. Watch your racquet head make contact with the shuttle before you look up. 2. Be sure to move into position and plant your back foot firmly before you begin your swing.

CRITERION TASK 4-3

Overhead Clear: Partner-Checked

Mark off 4 feet from the baseline of your opponent's court. Place cones or markers at that line (refer to Illustration 4.3). Stand in a good ready position around the middle of your court (X). Your partner will stand in the middle of the opposite court (P) and hit forehand drive clears to you with a high trajectory. If an incoming shot is not over your head, do not attempt to return it. Once your partner hits the shot to you, she or he should raise their racquet in the air overhead. Your clears should pass over your partner's raised racquet, indicating proper trajectory.

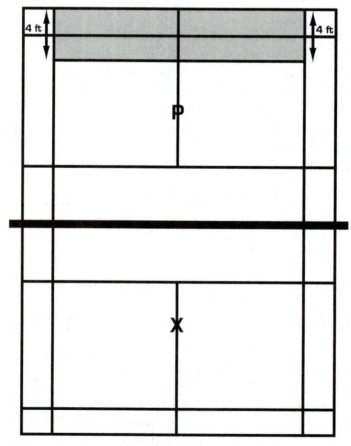

Illustration 4.3
Criterion Task 4-3

1. *Court position:* Middle
2. *Shuttle:* Forehand drive clears from your partner, standing at the center of her or his court; the shots must go over your head
3. *Trajectory:* Over outstretched racquet of your partner
4. *Aiming area:* Within 4 feet of opposite back boundary
5. *Criterion:* 6 of 10 with proper trajectory and landing in the aiming area. three sets.

Practice overhead clear returns of your partner's clears to the aiming area and with the proper trajectory. *If your partner's shot to you is not to your forehand side or cannot be hit with an overhead clear, do not count it.* Practice this task in blocks of 10 shots. Record the number of successful shots for each block on the **Personal Recording Form.** When your scores reach or exceed 6 out of 10 on three blocks, ask your partner to initial and date in the space provided.

Personal Recording Form									
Block 1	Block 2	Block 3	Block 4	Block 5	Block 6	Block 7	Block 8	Block 9	Block 10
___/10	___/10	___/10	___/10	___/10	___/10	___/10	___/10	___/10	___/10

Partner's initials _____   Date completed _____

CRITERION TASK 4-4

Clears: Instructor-Checked

Refer to Illustration 4.4.

Illustration 4.4
Criterion Task 4-4

1. *Court position:* Middle
2. *Shuttle:* Varied shots hit by your partner or instructor from the center of her or his court; you must return with an overhead clear or drive clear (forehand or backhand)
3. *Aiming area:* Within 4 feet of opposite back boundary
4. *Trajectory:* Over outstretched racquet of your partner or instructor
5. *Criterion:* 6 of 10 with proper trajectory and landing in the aiming area, two sets

Practice this task first with a partner, hitting blocks of 10 shots. When your block scores are consistently at or above 6 successful shots, ask your instructor to observe and witness your attempt at criterion. Once you have scored 6 or higher in two blocks, have your instructor initial and date in the space provided.

Personal Recording Form									
Block 1	Block 2	Block 3	Block 4	Block 5	Block 6	Block 7	Block 8	Block 9	Block 10
___/10	___/10	___/10	___/10	___/10	___/10	___/10	___/10	___/10	___/10

Instructor's initials _____ Date completed _____

CHALLENGE TASK FOR CLEARS

Find a partner who has also completed Criterion Task 4-4. Mark off lines on both sides of the court that extend from the singles side boundaries, 10 feet from the back boundary. This rectangle is the aiming area (see Illustration 4.5). Each partner (P-1 and P-2) must stand in the opposite aiming area to make shots. The purpose of this drill is to hit only overhead clears so that all shots *land in the aiming area and can be returned by your partner with an overhead clear*. Score 1 point each time the shuttle crosses the net with a high trajectory and can be returned by a partner from the aiming area. The objective is to see how many consecutive clears can be made by you and your partner. If a player must leave the defined area to hit a shot, the rally is over and the consecutive points stop. This is a team challenge, so try to hit clears that go to your partner's forehand side and have a high trajectory to let her or him make accurate returns. The challenge is over when you and your partner can score 10 points in a rally. Repeat this challenge with other players in your class.

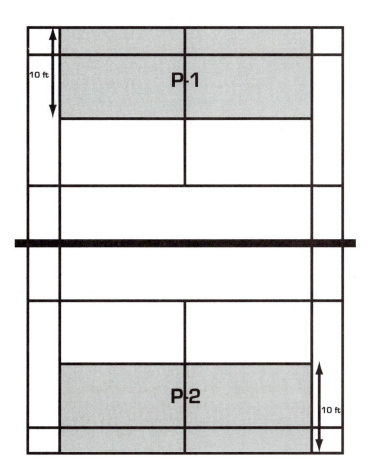

Illustration 4.5
Challenge Task for Clears

MODULE 5

DRIVE SHOTS

INTRODUCTION

Drives are usually attacking shots, used when your opponent is near one of the alleys on his or her side of the court. The objective is to take advantage of the opponent's extreme lateral position, aiming for the opposite side of his or her court, just inside the sideline. Drive shots have a medium trajectory and can be hit from either the forehand or backhand side. The strategy is to hit a shot that stays in the air for the shortest possible time and lands near the sideline, giving your opponent a long distance to cover in a very short time.

FOREHAND DRIVE

The forehand drive shot can be used when your opponent's shot comes to your forehand side, from any trajectory. You can make a forehand drive from any position on your side of the court, but it should not be used from the back part of your court when your opponent is near the net, leaving you vulnerable to a drop shot. It is always good strategy to aim your forehand drive shot to your opponent's backhand side when possible and to use it to move your opponent from the center area in his or her court.

INSTRUCTOR DEMONSTRATION

Your course instructor will provide you with an explanation and demonstration of the key performance cues for the forehand drive. If you have questions, be sure to ask them before proceeding to the individualized task sequence. Refer to Photos 5.1A through C as your instructor explains and demonstrates each performance cue for the forehand drive.

Photo 5.1A
Backswing, forehand drive

Photo 5.1B
Contact point, forehand drive

Photo 5.1C
Follow-through, forehand drive

PERFORMANCE CUES

1. **Court position:** Anywhere
2. **Aiming area:** Either opposite alley, within 3 feet of the side boundary
3. **Grip:** Forehand
4. **Footwork:** Forehand
5. **Contact point:** 3 o'clock (horizontal)
6. **Wrist action:** Full
7. **Trajectory:** Medium
8. **Power and speed:** Medium to full
9. **Follow-through:** Full

COMPREHENSION TASK

Find a partner and demonstrate to each other the proper performance cues for the forehand drive *without hitting the shuttle*. Be sure to provide feedback to each other for correct and incorrect performance cue, until both of you can execute this shot correctly.

LEARNING TIPS

1. This shot should be aimed only toward a side boundary. Never hit a drive to center court.
2. Hit this shot hard and fast, with a medium trajectory.
3. Aiming is important, so have your feet set and your front foot pointed to your aiming area.

READINESS DRILLS

5.1.   Stand in the center of your court. Beginning from the ready position, toss the shuttle to yourself on the forehand side and hit a drive shot. Be sure your toss is fully to your side. Do not toss it directly in front of yourself. At the start, do not be concerned with trajectory or accuracy; just begin to develop the proper techniques and consistency. Hit 40 forehand drives, or continue this task until you can consistently hit shots with the proper power and trajectory.

5.2.   Repeat the previous task, but this time have a partner stand in the center of the opposite court and gently hit shuttles to your forehand side. Be sure you start from the ready position at the center of your court for all shots. You will need to move into proper position to make your shots. Again, do not be concerned with power or accuracy at the beginning. Work on moving into position and using the proper techniques with consistency. Hit 40 forehand drives, or continue this task until you can consistently hit shots with the proper power and trajectory.

If you experience difficulty with the readiness drill, refer to the **Performance Cues** and review each cue as presented. If you still have difficulty, ask your course instructor to assist you in applying these techniques.

Common Errors and Their Correction

Error	Correction
Not enough power.	1. Be sure to plant your back foot and step into the shot. 2. Use more power and a full wrist action on the swing.
Low trajectory.	1. Contact point too low. 2. Be sure to complete the follow-through at eye level.
Poor contact (no control).	1. Watch your racquet head make contact with the shuttle before you look up. 2. Be sure to move into position and plant your back foot firmly before you begin your swing.

CRITERION TASK 5-1

Forehand Drive: Partner-Checked

Find a partner and set up a court with cones or markers placed 3 feet inside the opposite right singles alley (see illustration 5.1). Assume a good ready position in the middle area of your court (X). Your partner (P) will stand in the middle area of his or her court and hit soft, medium-trajectory shots (serves or drives) to your forehand side. You may have to move to get in the proper position for some shots, so be ready. You should hit forehand drive shots with a low to medium trajectory that land in the aiming area.

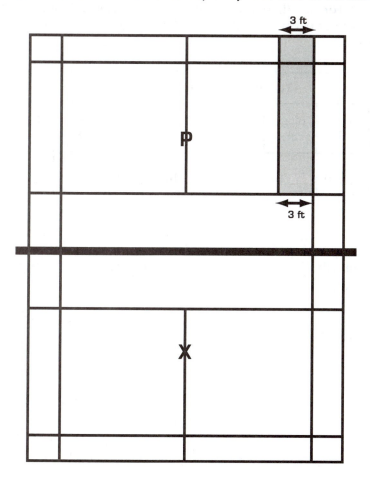

Illustration 5.1
Criterion Task 5-1

1. *Court position:* Middle
2. *Shuttle:* "Served" from your partner, standing at the center of his or her court; shots must come to your forehand side with a medium trajectory
3. *Trajectory:* Medium
4. *Aiming area:* Within 3 feet of the opposite singles side boundary on your forehand side
5. *Criterion:* 7 of 10 with proper trajectory and landing in aiming area, four sets

Practice forehand drive returns of your partner's shots to the aiming area and with the proper trajectory. *If his or her shot is not to your forehand side or cannot be hit with a drive, do not count it.* Practice this task in blocks of 10 shots. Record the number of successful shots for each block on the **Personal Recording Form**. When your scores reach or exceed 7 out of 10 on four blocks, ask your partner to initial and date in the space provided.

Personal Recording Form									
Block 1	Block 2	Block 3	Block 4	Block 5	Block 6	Block 7	Block 8	Block 9	Block 10
___/10	___/10	___/10	___/10	___/10	___/10	___/10	___/10	___/10	___/10

Partner's initials _____ Date completed _____

BACKHAND DRIVE

The backhand drive shot can be used when your opponent's shot comes to your backhand side, from any trajectory. You can make a backhand drive from any position on your side of the court, but it should not be used from the back part of your court when your opponent is near the net, leaving you vulnerable to a drop shot. It is always good strategy to aim your backhand drive shot to your opponents' backhand side when possible and to use it to move your opponent from the center area in his or her court.

INSTRUCTOR DEMONSTRATION

Your course instructor will provide you with an explanation and demonstration of the key performance cues for the backhand drive. If you have questions, be sure to ask them before proceeding to the individualized task sequence. Refer to Photos 5.2A through C as your instructor explains and demonstrates each performance cue for the backhand drive.

Photo 5.2A
Backswing, backhand drive

Photo 5.2B
Contact point, backhand drive

Photo 5.2C
Follow-through, backhand drive

PERFORMANCE CUES

1. **Court position:** Anywhere
2. **Aiming area:** Either opposite alley, within 3 feet of the side boundary
3. **Grip:** Backhand
4. **Footwork:** Backhand
5. **Contact point:** 9 o'clock (horizontal)
6. **Wrist action:** Full
7. **Trajectory:** Medium
8. **Power and speed:** Medium to full
9. **Follow-through:** Full

COMPREHENSION TASK

Find a partner and demonstrate to each other the proper performance cues for the backhand drive without *hitting the shuttle*. Be sure to provide feedback to each other for correct and incorrect performance cues until both of you can execute this shot correctly.

LEARNING TIPS

1. This shot should be aimed only toward a side boundary. Never hit a drive to center court.
2. Hit this shot hard and fast, with a medium trajectory.
3. Aiming is important, so have your feet set and your front foot pointed to your aiming area.
4. Keep your striking arm elbow close to your body. Do not lead with your elbow.

READINESS DRILLS

5.3. Stand in the center of your court. Beginning from the ready position, toss the shuttle to yourself on the backhand side and hit a drive shot. Be sure your toss is fully to your side. Do not toss it directly in front of yourself. At the start, do not be concerned with trajectory or accuracy; just begin to develop the proper techniques and consistency. Hit 40 backhand drives, or continue this task until you can consistently hit shots with the proper power and trajectory.

5.4. Repeat this task with a partner standing in the center of the opposite court and gently hitting shuttles to your backhand side. Be sure you start from the ready position at the center of your court for all shots. You will need to move into proper position to make your shots. Again, do not be concerned with power or accuracy at the beginning. Work on moving into position and using the proper techniques with consistency. Hit 40 backhand drives, or continue this task until you can consistently hit shots with the proper power and trajectory.

If you experience difficulty with the readiness drill, refer to the **Performance Cues** and review each cue as presented. If you still have difficulty, ask your course instructor to assist you in applying these techniques.

Common Errors and Their Correction

Error	Correction
Not enough power.	1. Be sure to plant your back foot and step into the shot.
	2. Use more power and a full wrist action on the swing.
Low trajectory.	1. Contact point too low.
	2. Be sure to complete the follow-through at eye level.
Poor contact (no control).	1. Watch your racquet head make contact with the shuttle before you look up.
	2. Be sure to move into position and plant your back foot firmly before you begin your swing.

CRITERION TASK 5-2

Backhand Drive: Partner-Checked

Find a partner and set up a court with cones or markers placed 4 feet inside the singles boundary to denote the opposite left singles alley (see Illustration 5.2). You will assume a good ready position in the middle area of your court (X). Your partner (P) will stand in the middle area of his or her court and hit soft, medium trajectory shots (serves or drives) to your backhand side. You may have to move to get in the proper position for some shots, so be ready. You should hit backhand drive shots with a low to medium trajectory that land in the aiming area.

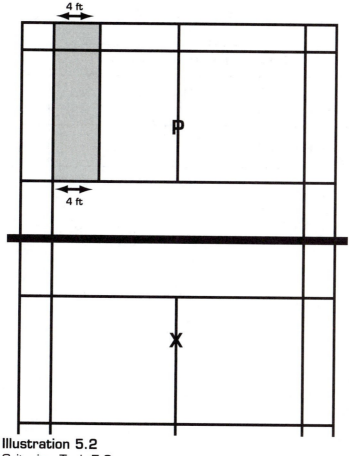

Illustration 5.2
Criterion Task 5-2

1. *Court position:* Middle
2. *Shuttle:* "Served" from your partner, standing at the center of his or her court; shots must come to your backhand side with a medium trajectory
3. *Trajectory:* Medium
4. *Aiming area:* Within 4 feet of singles side boundary on your backhand side
5. *Criterion:* 6 of 10 with proper trajectory and landing in aiming area, three sets

Practice backhand drive returns of your partner's serves to the aiming area and with the proper trajectory. *If his or her shot is not to your backhand side or cannot be hit with a drive, do not count it.* Practice this task in blocks of 10 shots. Record the number of successful shots for each block on the **Personal Recording Form**. When your scores reach or exceed 6 out of 10 on three blocks, ask your partner to initial and datre in the space provided.

Personal Recording Form									
Block 1	Block 2	Block 3	Block 4	Block 5	Block 6	Block 7	Block 8	Block 9	Block 10
___/10	___/10	___/10	___/10	___/10	___/10	___/10	___/10	___/10	___/10

Partner's initials _____ Date completed _____

CRITERION TASK 5-3

Drive Shots: Instructor-Checked

Refer to Illustration 5.3

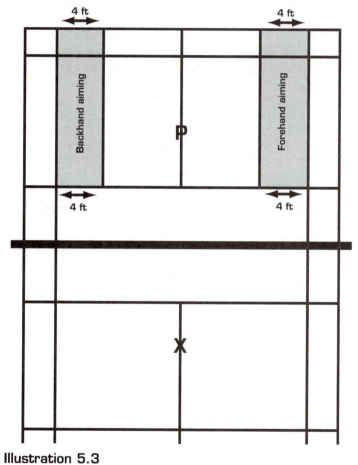

Illustration 5.3
Criterion Task 5-3

1. *Court position:* Middle (X)
2. *Shuttle:* "Served" from your partner or instructor (P), standing at the center of his or her court; shots can come to your forehand or backhand side, with no advanced indication
3. *Trajectory:* Medium
4. *Aiming area:* Within 4 feet of correct side boundary
5. *Criterion:* 6 of 10 with proper trajectory and landing in correct aiming area, two sets.

Practice this task first with a partner, hitting blocks of 10 shots. **For forehand shots, the correct aiming area is the alley to your right. For backhand shots, the correct aiming area is the alley to your left. (Reverse this for left-handed players.)** When your block scores are consistently at or above 6 out of 10, ask your instructor to observe and witness your attempt at criterion. Once you have scored 6 or higher on two blocks, have your instructor initial and date in the space provided.

Personal Recording Form									
Block 1	Block 2	Block 3	Block 4	Block 5	Block 6	Block 7	Block 8	Block 9	Block 10
___/10	___/10	___/10	___/10	___/10	___/10	___/10	___/10	___/10	___/10

Instructor's initials _____   Date completed _____

MODULE **6**

OVERHEAD SMASHES

INTRODUCTION

Smashes are always attacking shots, hit with the overhead technique. The objective is to hit a hard shot, aimed directly at the floor on your opponent's side, so that it cannot be returned in any fashion. For beginners, smashes should be hit only from the forehand side when the shuttle enters your middle court area with a high trajectory, usually when your opponent's clear has fallen short. Because smashes are hit with maximum power, they are not likely to be as accurate as drives or clears, so it is important not to aim too close to the net or any boundary with this shot.

INSTRUCTOR DEMONSTRATION

Your course instructor will provide you with an explanation and demonstration of the key performance cues for the overhead smash shot. If you have questions, be sure to ask them before proceeding to the individualized task sequence. Refer to Photos 6.1A through C as your instructor explains and demonstrates each of the performance cues for the overhead smash.

Photo 6.1A
Backswing, overhead smash

Photo 6.1B
Contact point, overhead smash

Photo 6.1C
Follow-through, overhead smash

PERFORMANCE CUES

1. **Court position:** Anywhere, but smashes are more effective from the middle and front areas
2. **Aiming areas:** To an alley (but not too close to the side boundary) or to any part of the opposite court away from your opponent; opponent's backhand side preferred
3. **Grip:** Forehand
4. **Footwork:** Forehand, with upright position and short stride
5. **Contact point:** 1 o'clock (moving downward)
6. **Wrist action:** Full, downward
7. **Trajectory:** Straight line down from contact point to aiming area
8. **Power and speed:** Full
9. **Follow-through:** Full, downward

COMPREHENSION TASK

Find a partner and demonstrate to each other the proper performance cues for the overhead smash *without hitting the shuttle*. Be sure to provide feedback to each other for correct and incorrect performance cues until both of you can execute this shot correctly.

LEARNING TIPS

1. Be sure to get your feet set and watch the shuttle all the way to the contact point. Do not get too anxious!
2. This is a power shot, but controlled accuracy is still important. Concentrate on placement when practicing.

READINESS DRILLS

6.1. Starting from the ready position, toss the shuttle high to yourself on your forehand side. It may take a few tries to get the toss correct. When you can get the toss correct, work on getting the correct contact point and hitting the shuttle hard to the floor. Do not be concerned with accuracy at this time. Do this task until you make consistently good contact and hit the shuttle directly to the floor about 10 feet in front of you.

6.2. Stand in the ready position at the intersection of the short service line and center service line. Have a partner hit **high, short** serves to your forehand side. Move into position and hit smashes to the opposite court. Do not be concerned with accuracy at this time; work to make consistent contact with a straight trajectory. Do this 30 times or until you are consistent. Once you are consistent from that spot, move back about 6 feet and repeat the same task.

If you experience difficulty with the readiness drill, refer to the **Performance Cues** and review each cue as presented. If you still have difficulty, ask your course instructor to assist you in applying these techniques.

Common Errors and Their Correction

Error	**Correction**
Making contact on the rim of the racquet.	1. Be sure to watch the shuttle all the way to the contact point of your swing. 2. Move to get set all the way under the shuttle before you start your swing. 3. Take a short step for this shot.
Incorrect trajectory (into the net or too long).	Be sure to get set under the shuttle and make contact at 1 o'clock, hitting **downward.**
Lack of power. The shuttle floats across the net.	1. Make contact at 1 o'clock hitting **downward.** 2. Swing harder with full follow-through.
Shots go too far to the right or left.	Be sure to have your lead foot pointing to your aiming area. Do not hit across your body.

CRITERION TASK 6-1

Overhead Smashes: Partner-Checked

Get in a good ready position at the middle of your court (X). Your partner will stand in the middle of the opposite court (P), and hit high, short serves to your forehand side. Your aiming area is the entire right side of the singles area in the opposite court. Refer to Illustration 6.1.

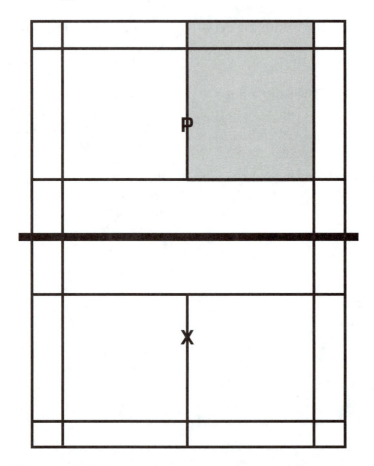

Illustration 6.1
Criterion Task 6-1

1. *Position:* Middle of your court, in ready position
2. *Aiming area:* Opposite singles service area on your forehand side
3. *Trajectory:* Downward from contact point to aiming area
4. *Shuttle:* High "serves" hit from your partner to your forehand side
5. *Criterion:* 8 of 10 smashes into the aiming area, 3 sets

Practice smash returns of your partner's serves to the aiming area and with the proper downward trajectory. *If his or her shot is not to your forehand side or cannot be hit with a smash, do not count it.* Practice this task in blocks of 10 shots. Record the number of successful shots for each block on the **Personal Recording Form**. When your scores reach or exceed 8 out of 10 on three blocks, ask your partner to initial and date in the space provided.

Personal Recording Form									
Block 1	Block 2	Block 3	Block 4	Block 5	Block 6	Block 7	Block 8	Block 9	Block 10
__/10	__/10	__/10	__/10	__/10	__/10	__/10	__/10	__/10	__/10

Partner's initials _____ Date completed _____

MODULE 7

DROP SHOTS

INTRODUCTION

Drops shots can be either attacking or defensive shots. They are very similar to the low short serve you have already learned. A drop shot should cross low over the net and be aimed to the very front of your opponent's`court. It is very important that your drop shot does not go too high or too deep, allowing your opponent an easy opportunity for a smash return, for which you will have little defense. Drop shots can be made from either the forehand or backhand side.

FOREHAND DROP

The forehand drop shot is hit with a light lifting motion, as if you were trying to set the shuttle on a shelf. You should try to get this shot over the net with as little clearance as possible, landing in the very front of your opponent's court, giving him or her less time to devise an effective return. While it is always advisable to hit the drop shot to your opponent's backhand side, it should be played over the net as quickly as you can, regardless of which side, to have an element of surprise and to reduce reaction time.

INSTRUCTOR DEMONSTRATION

Your course instructor will provide you with an explanation and demonstration of the key performance cues for the forehand drop shot. If you have questions, be sure to ask them before proceeding to the individualized task sequence. Refer to Photos 7.1A through C as your instructor explains and demonstrates each of the performance cues for the forehand drop.

Photo 7.1A
Backswing, forehand drop shot

Photo 7.1B
Contact point, forehand drop shot

Photo 7.1C
Follow-through, forehand drop shot

PERFORMANCE CUES

1. **Court position:** In front half of your court
2. **Aiming area:** Between the net and opposite short service line, backhand side preferred
3. **Grip:** Forehand or underhand
4. **Footwork:** Forehand, with extended stride
5. **Contact point:** Between 3 and 4 o'clock, moving upward
6. **Wrist action:** Firm
7. **Trajectory:** Low, close to the net
8. **Power and speed:** Low
9. **Follow-through:** Short, with upward lifting action

COMPREHENSION TASK

Find a partner and demonstrate to each other the proper performance cues for the forehand drop *without hitting the shuttle.* Be sure to provide feedback to each other for correct and incorrect performance cues until both of you can execute this shot correctly.

LEARNING TIPS

1. A low trajectory and aiming area near the net are critical. If the shuttle is popped up or goes too deep into your opponent's court, you will be susceptible to a smash return.
2. Make this shot as soft as you can by using a slow lifting action with a firm wrist and short stroke.
3. This shot is very similar to the low short serve you have already learned. the major difference is that your aiming area is in front of the short service line, not over it.

READINESS DRILL

7.1.   Position yourself at the serving spot of your choice. Drop the shuttle to yourself as you would for a low short serve. Using the low short serve technique, hit drop shots that clear the net with a low trajectory and land in front of the opposite short service line. Do not be concerned with specific placement to the forehand or backhand side. Do this 30 times or until you can consistently hit correct drop shots from the serving position.

If you experience difficulty with the readiness drill, refer to the **Performance Cues** and review each cue as presented. If you still have difficulty, ask your course instructor to assist you in applying these techniques.

Common Errors and Their Correction

Error	Correction
The shuttle is popped up.	Be sure to use a lifting action, with a firm wrist and short follow-through.
Shuttle is hit into the net.	1. Check your position. Do not get too close to the net. 2. Check your contact point. It should be at 3 o'clock, moving almost directly upward.
Making contact on the rim of the racquet.	1. Be sure to plant your back foot before striding to make the shot. 2. Be sure to watch the shuttle, not your aiming area.

CRITERION TASK 7-1

Forehand Drop Shot: Partner-Checked

Stand in a good ready position in the middle of your court (X). Your partner will be in the right serving area of the opposite court (P), hitting low, short serves to your forehand side. Your aiming area is the rectangle in front of the left serving box on the opposite side. Remember, if the shuttle hits the top of the net and falls into the aiming area, it is "good." You will need to anticipate moving into the proper position to make your drop shots. Refer to Illustration 7.1

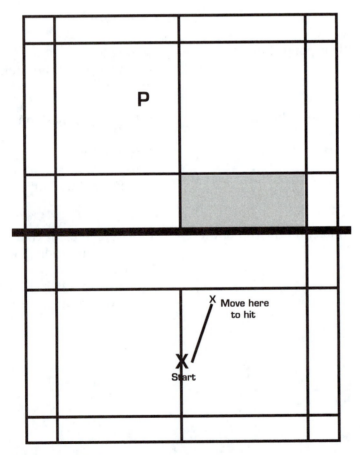

Illustration 7.1
Criterion Task 7-1

1. *Position:* Ready position, in middle of the court
2. *Aiming area:* Over the net, in front of short service line to your forehand side
3. *Trajectory:* Low, just over the net
4. *Shuttle:* Short low serves hit by your partner to your forehand side. You must move into position to make your drop shots as the shuttle comes to your side of the court. This task is not being done correctly if you are hitting your shots without moving from your initial position.
5. *Criterion:* 8 of 10 forehand drop shots into aiming area, two sets

Practice forehand drop returns of your partner's serves into the aiming area and with the proper trajectory. *If his or her serve is not to your forehand side or cannot be hit with a drop shot, do not count it.* Practice this task in blocks of 10 shots. Record the number of successful shots for each block on the Personal Recording Form. When your scores reach or exceed 8 out of 10 on two blocks, ask your partner to initial and date in the space provided.

Personal Recording Form									
Block 1	Block 2	Block 3	Block 4	Block 5	Block 6	Block 7	Block 8	Block 9	Block 10
___/10	___/10	___/10	___/10	___/10	___/10	___/10	___/10	___/10	___/10

Partner's initials _____   Date completed _____

BACKHAND DROP

The backhand drop shot has the same strategic use as the forehand drop shot. It can be either a defensive or an attacking shot. You should try to get this shot over the net with as little clearance as possible, landing in the very front of your opponent's court, giving him or her less time to devise an effective return. In one sense, the decision to make the backhand drop shot is determined by your opponent. When you are given a short shot to your backhand side near the net, usually your only option will be to use this shot. This is an important shot to master because you can anticipate that your opponent will try to hit many shots to your backhand side (just as you will try to do to him or her), so you are likely to use the backhand drop shot often in a match.

INSTRUCTOR DEMONSTRATION

Your course instructor will provide you with an explanation and demonstration of the key performance cues for the backhand drop shot. If you have questions, be sure to ask them before proceeding to the individualized task sequence. Refer to Photos 7.2A through C as your instructor explains and demonstrates each of the performance cues for the backhand drop.

Photo 7.2A
Backswing, backhand drop shot

Photo 7.2B
Contact point, backhand
drop shot

Photo 7.2C
Follow-through, backhand drop shot

PERFORMANCE CUES

1. **Court position:** In front half of your court
2. **Aiming area:** Between the net and opposite short service line, backhand side preferred
3. **Grip:** Backhand
4. **Footwork:** Backhand, with extended stride
5. **Contact point:** 3 o'clock, upward
6. **Wrist action:** Firm
7. **Trajectory:** Low, close to the net
8. **Power and speed:** Low
9. **Follow-through:** Short, upward lifting action

COMPREHENSION TASK

Find a partner and demonstrate to each other the proper performance cues for the backhand drop *without hitting the shuttle.* Be sure to provide feedback to each other for correct and incorrect performance cues until both of you can execute this shot correctly.

LEARNING TIPS

1. A low trajectory and aiming area near the net are critical. If the shuttle is popped up or goes too deep into your opponent's court, you will be susceptible to a smash return by your opponent, probably from his or her forehand side.
2. Make this shot as soft as you can by using a slow lifting action with a firm wrist and short stroke

READINESS DRILL

7-2. Position yourself just behind the short service line. Starting from the ready position, toss the shuttle to yourself on your backhand side. You may need to practice the toss a few times to become consistent. Using the backhand drop shot technique, hit shots that clear the net with a low trajectory and land in front of the opposite short service line. Do not be concerned with specific placement to the forehand or backhand side. Do this 30 times or until you can consistently hit correct backhand drop shots from the ready position.

If you experience difficulty with the readiness drill, refer to the **Performance Cues** and review each cue as presented. If you still have difficulty, ask your course instructor to assist you in applying these techniques.

Common Errors and Their Correction

Error	Correction
The shuttle is popped up.	Be sure to use a lifting action, with a firm wrist and short follow-through.
Shuttle is hit into the net.	1. Check your position. Do not get too close to the net. 2. Check your contact point. It should be at 3 o'clock, moving almost directly upward.
Making contact on the rim of the racquet.	1. Be sure to plant your back foot before striding to make the shot. 2. Be sure to watch the shuttle, not your aiming area.

CRITERION TASK 7-2

Backhand Drop Shots: Instructor-Checked

Stand in a good ready position in the middle of your court (X). Your partner (or the instructor) will be in the left serving area of the opposite court (P), hitting low, short serves to your backhand side. Your aiming area is the rectangle in front of the right serving box on the opposite side. Remember, if the shuttle hits the top of the net and falls into the aiming area, it is "good." You will need to anticipate moving into the proper position to make your drop shots. Refer to Illustration 7.2.

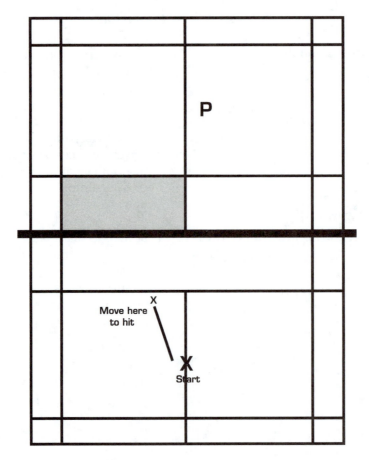

Illustration 7.2
Criterion Task 7-2

1. *Position:* Ready position, in middle of the court
2. *Aiming area:* Over the net, in front of the short service line to your backhand side
3. *Trajectory:* Low, close to the net
4. *Shuttle:* Short low serves hit by your partner to your backhand side. You must move into position to make your drop shots as the shuttle comes to your side of the court. *This task is not being done correctly if you are hitting your shots without moving from your initial position.*
5. *Criterion:* 7 of 10 backhand drop shots into aiming area, two sets.

Practice backhand drop returns of your partner's serves into the aiming area and with the proper trajectory. *If his or her serve is not to your backhand side or cannot be hit with a drop shot, do not count it.* Practice this task in blocks of 10 shots. Record the number of successful shots for each block on the **Personal Recording Form**. When your scores reach or exceed 7 out of 10 on two blocks, ask your instructor to initial and date in the space provided.

Personal Recording Form									
Block 1	Block 2	Block 3	Block 4	Block 5	Block 6	Block 7	Block 8	Block 9	Block 10
___/10	___/10	___/10	___/10	___/10	___/10	___/10	___/10	___/10	___/10

Instructor's initials _____ Date completed _____

CHALLENGE TASK

Serving and Returning Serves

Find a partner who has also finished Criterion Task 7-2. This challenge task will give you both practice on making and returning serves, now that you know two kinds of serves and several shots used to return serves. Mark off the court as shown in Illustration 7.2. This defines the middle court area. Each partner will serve in alternating turns. The other partner should be positioned in the appropriate service return box, in the ready position. The server (S) can use a low short serve or a high deep serve. Once the serve is made, the server must remain in the marked middle court area; but can reach outside the box to make his or her next shot. The returner (R) is free to move anywhere in the service return box to make the return attempt. The server's objective is to force the returner to hit the shuttle back to the middle area. The returner's objective is to return the serve within the singles boundary in an area other than the middle.

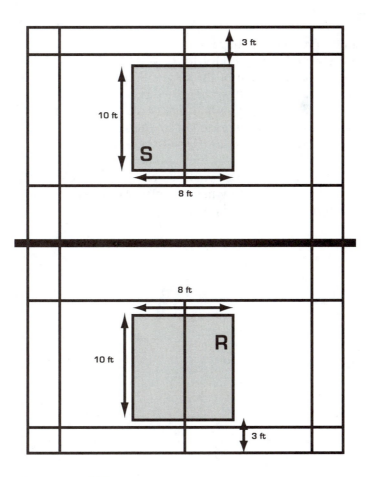

Illustration 7.3
Challenge Task for Serving and Returning Serves

SCORING

1. Any fault serve (score 1 for returner)
2. Any nonreturned serve (score 1 for server)
3. Any return that lands out of the singles boundaries (score 1 for server)
4. Any serve that is returned so that the server can strike it from the middle area, *regardless of the result of that shot* (score 1 for server)
5. Any return that cannot be reached by the server from inside the middle area, *but is otherwise in bounds* (score 1 for returner)

Note that a point is given on all serves, with the scoring based on shot accuracy. The challenge is over when one player reaches 10 points. Repeat the challenge with several other players in class.

MODULE **8**

LAWS OF BADMINTON
AND GAME STRATEGY

Having just completed the **Performance Skills Modules** of PSIS badminton, we now turn to this **Badminton Knowledge Module,** which will teach you the basic rules and strategy of badminton. The Badminton Knowledge Module can be completed in just one or two class periods. If you have more days than that remaining until the end of the term, you can play matches with your classmates, review the final Criterion Task in each module, or ask your instructor to teach you some advanced badminton shots. You can use your remaining classes to refine your basic skills or to develop competitive skills for badminton singles and doubles.

INTRODUCTION

Most of you are familiar with "backyard badminton" played with a high net, low-quality equipment, and rules set by mutual agreement of players It is fun, but very different from the game played at a competitive level in compliance with established rules (or laws) by skilled players (such as yourself after completing the Performance Skills Modules of PSIS badminton). To really appreciate the game of badminton and enjoy its many benefits, you must learn to play it in a standard version, against opponents of equal or slightly better skill than your own. In this version, badminton is a vigorous game with subtle tactical nuances that will challenge your skills and competitive abilities, bringing you a high level of satisfying participation for a lifetime. Now that you have learned some beginning badminton skills, this unit will help you learn the game of competitive badminton.

READING ASSIGNMENT

Take time to carefully read the following Laws of Badminton and the section on badminton strategy. As you read, make marginal notes on items that are not clear to you. The next day in class ask your instructor to provide a longer explanation of these items or, better yet, a *demonstration*. Many of the laws and strategies can be best understood by seeing and hearing how they are interpreted and applied.

When you have finished the reading and have no more questions for your instructor, complete the brief Badminton Knowledge Quiz at the end of this module. If the quiz will be used for grading, your instructor will inform you about how it will be evaluated. If this quiz will not be used for grading, we recommend that you score at least 80% and have your instructor review missed answers with you. In this way, you will have a good working knowledge of badminton laws and strategy before you begin competitive play in class or on your own.

LAWS OF BADMINTON

1. COURT

1.1   The court shall be a rectangle and laid out as in Illustration 1, defined by lines 1" (40 mm) wide.

1.2   The lines shall be easily distinguishable and preferably be colored white or yellow.

    1.3.1   To show the zone in which a shuttle of correct pace lands when tested (Law 4.4), an additional four marks 1" by 1" (40 mm by 40 mm) may be made inside each side line for singles of the right service court, 1' 9" (530 mm) to 3' 3" (990 mm) from the back boundary line.

    1.3.2   In making these marks, their width shall be within the measurement given, i.e., the marks will be from 1' 9" (530 mm) to 1' 10" (570 mm) and from 3' 1" (950 mm) to 3' 3" (990 mm) from the outside of the back boundary line.

1.4   All lines form part of the area which they define.

1.5   Where space does not permit the marking out of a court for doubles, a court may be marked out for singles only. The back boundary lines become also the long service lines, and the posts, or the strips or material representing them (Law 2.2), shall be placed on the side lines.

2. POSTS

2.1   The posts shall be 5' 1" (1.55 m) in height from the surface of the court. They shall be sufficiently firm to remain vertical and keep the net strained as provided in Law 3, and shall be placed on the doubles side lines.

2.2   Where it is not practicable to have posts on the side lines, some method must be used to indicate the position of the side lines where they pass under the net, e.g., by the use of thin posts or strips of material 1" (40 mm) wide, fixed to the side lines and rising vertically to the net cord.

2.3   On a court marked for doubles, the posts or strips of material representing the posts shall be placed on the side lines for doubles, regardless of whether singles or doubles is being played.

3. NET

3.1   The net shall be made of fine cord of dark color and even thickness with a mesh not less than 1mm and not more than 2mm.
3.2   The net shall be 2' 6" (760 mm) in depth.
3.3   The top of the net shall be edged with a 3" (75 mm) white tape doubled over a cord or cable running through the tape. This tape must rest upon the cord or cable.
3.4   The cord or cable shall be of sufficient size and weight to be firmly stretched flush with the top of the posts.
3.5   The top of the net from the surface of the court shall be 5' (1,524 m) at the center of the court and 5' 1" (1.55 m) over the side lines for doubles.
3.6   There shall be no gaps between the ends of the net and the posts. If necessary, the full depth of the net should be tied at the ends.

4. SHUTTLE

Principles—The shuttle may be made from natural and/or synthetic materials. Whatever material the shuttle is made from, the flight characteristics, generally, should be similar to those produced by a natural feathered shuttle with a cork base covered by a thin layer of leather. Having regard to the Principles:

4.1   General Design
    4.1.1 The shuttle shall have 16 feathers fixed in the base.
    4.1.2 The feathers can have a variable length from 2" (64 mm) to 2" (70 mm), but in each shuttle they shall all be the same length when measured from the tip to the top of the base.
    4.1.3 The tips of the feathers shall form a circle with a diameter from 2" (58 mm) to 2 5/8" (68 mm).
    4.1.4 The feathers shall be fastened firmly with thread or other suitable material.

4.1.5 The base shall be:
* 1" (25 mm) to 1 1/8" (28 mm) in diameter
* round on the bottom.

4.2 Weight. The shuttle shall weigh from 4.74 to 5.50 grams.

4.3 Non-Feathered Shuttle

4.3.1 The skirt, or simulation of feathers in synthetic materials, replaces natural feathers.

4.3.2 The base is described in Law 4.1.5.

4.3.3 Measurements and weight shall be as in Laws 4.1.2, 4.1.3 and 4.2. However, because of the difference of the specific gravity and behavior of synthetic materials in comparison with feathers, a variation of up to 10 percent is acceptable.

4.4 Shuttle Testing

4.4.1 To test a shuttle, use a full underhand stroke which makes contact with the shuttle over the back boundary line. The shuttle shall be hit at an upward angle and in a direction parallel to the side lines.

4.4.2 A shuttle of correct pace will land not less than 1' 9" (530 mm) and not more than 3'-3" (990 mm) short of the other back boundary line.

4.5 Modifications

Subject to there being no variation in the general design, pace and flight of the shuttle, modifications in the above specifications may be made with the approval of the National Organization concerned:

4.5.1 In places where atmospheric conditions due to either altitude or climate make the standard shuttle unsuitable; or

4.5.2 In special circumstances which make it otherwise necessary in the interests of the game.

5. RACQUET

5.1 The hitting surface of the racquet shall be flat and consist of a pattern of crossed strings connected to a frame and either alternately interlaced or bonded where they cross. The stringing pattern shall be generally uniform and, in particular, not less dense in the center than in any other area.

5.2 The frame of the racquet, including the handle, shall not exceed 2' 2" (680 mm) in overall length and 9" (230 mm) in overall width.

5.3 The overall length of the head shall not exceed 11 3/8" (290 mm).

5.4 The strung surface shall not exceed 11" (280 mm) in overall length and 8 5/8" (220 mm) in overall width.

5.5 The racquet:

5.5.1 Shall be free of attached objects and protrusions, other than those utilized solely and specifically to limit wear and tear, or vibration, or to distribute weight, or to secure the handle by cord to the player's hand, and which are reasonable in size and placement for such purposes; and

5.5.2 Shall be free of any device which makes it possible for a player to change materially the shape of the racquet.

6. APPROVED EQUIPMENT

The International Badminton Federation shall rule on any question of whether any racquet, shuttle or equipment or any prototype used in the playing of badminton complies with the specifications or is otherwise approved or not approved for play. Such ruling may be undertaken on the federation's initiative or upon application by any party with a bona fide interest therein including any player, equipment manufacturer or National Organization or member thereof.

7. PLAYERS

7.1 "Player" applies to all those taking part in a match.

7.2 The game shall be played, in the case of doubles, by two players a side, or in the case of singles, by one player a side.

7.3 The side having the right to serve shall be called the serving side, and the opposing side shall be called the receiving side.

8. TOSS

8.1 Before commencing play, the opposing sides shall toss and the side winning the toss shall exercise the choice in either Law 8.1.1 or Law 8.1.2.

8.1.1 To serve or receive first.

          8.1.2 To start play at one end of the court or the other.

8.2   The side losing the toss shall then exercise the remaining choice.

9. SCORING

9.1   The opposing sides shall play the best of three games unless otherwise arranged. It is permissible to play one game of 21 points by prior arrangement.

9.2   Only the serving side can add points to its score.

9.3   In doubles and Men's singles a game is won by the first side to score 15 points (21 points in a match consisting of a single game to 21 points), except as provided in Law 9.6.

9.4   In women's singles a game is won by the first side to score 11 points, except as provided by Law 9.6.

          9.5.1 If the score becomes 13 or 14 all (9 or 10 all in Women's singles) (19 or 20 in a 21 point game) the side which first scored 13 or 14 (9 or 10) (19 or 20) shall have the choice of "setting" or "not setting" the game (Law 9.6).

          9.5.2 This choice can only be made when the score is first reached and must be made before the next service is delivered.

          9.5.3 The relevant side (Law 9.5.1) is given the opportunity to set at 14 all (10 all in Women's singles) (20 all in a 21 point game) despite any previous decision not to set by that side or the opposing side at 13 all (9 all in Women's singles)(19 all in a 21 point game).

9.6   If the game has been set, the score is called "love all" and the side first scoring the set number of points (Laws 9.6.1 to 9.6.4) wins the game.

          9.6.1 13 all setting to 5 points

          9.6.2 14 all setting to 3 points

          9.6.3 9 all setting to 3 points

          9.6.4 10 all setting to 2 points

          9.6.5 19 all setting to 5 points

          9.6.6 20 all setting to 3 points

9.7   The side winning a game serves first in the next game.

10. CHANGE OF ENDS

10.1 Players shall change ends:

         10.1.1 At the end of the first game;

10.1.2 Prior to the beginning of the third game (if any); and

10.1.3 In the third game, or in a one game match, when the leading score reaches:
* 6 in a game of 11 points
* 8 in a game of 15 points
* 11 in a game of 21 points

10.2 When the players omit to change ends as indicated by Law 10.1, theyshall do so immediately the mistake is discovered and the existing score shall stand.

11. SERVICE

11.1 In a correct service:

11.1.1 Neither side shall cause undue delay to the delivery of the serve.

11.1.2 The server and receiver shall stand within diagonally opposite service courts without touching the boundary lines of these service courts; some part of both feet of the server and receiver must remain in contact with the surface of the court in a stationary position until the service is delivered (Law 11.4);

11.1.3 The server's racquet shall initially hit the base of the shuttle while the whole of the shuttle is below the server's waist;

11.1.4 The shaft of the server's racquet at the instant of hitting the shuttle shall be pointing in a downward direction to such an extent that the whole of the head of the racquet is discernible below the whole of the server's hand holding the racquet;

11.1.5 The movement of the server's racquet must continue forwards after the start of the service (Law 11.2) until the service is delivered; and

11.1.6 The flight of the shuttle shall be upwards from the server's racquet to pass over the net, so that, if not intercepted, it falls in the receiver's service court.

11.2 Once the players have taken their positions, the first forward movement of the server's racquet is the start of the service.

11.3 The server shall not serve before the receiver is ready, but the receiver shall be considered to have been ready if a return of service is attempted.

11.4 The service is delivered when, once started (Law 11.2), the shuttle is hit by the server's racquet or the shuttle lands on the floor.

11.5 In doubles, the partners may take up any positions which do not unsight the opposing server or receiver.

12. SINGLES

12.1 The players shall serve from, and receive in, their respective right service courts when the server has not scored or has scored an even number of points in that game.

12.2 The players shall serve from, and receive in, their respective left service courts when the server has not scored or has scored an odd number of points in that game.

12.3 If a game is set, the total points scored by the server in that game shall be used to apply Laws 12.1 and 12.2.

12.4 The shuttle is hit alternately by the server and the receiver until a "fault" is made or the shuttle ceases to be in play.

12.5.1 If the receiver makes a "fault" or the shuttle ceases to be in play because it touches the surface of the court inside the receiver's court, the server scores a point. The server then serves again from the alternate service court.

12.5.2 If the server makes a "fault" or the shuttle ceases to be in play because it touches the surface of the court inside the server's court, the server loses the right to continue serving, and the receiver then becomes the server, with no point scored by either player.

13. DOUBLES

13.1 At the start of a game, and each time a side gains the right to serve, the service shall be delivered from the right service court.

13.2 Only the receiver shall return the service: should the shuttle touch or be hit by the receiver's partner, the serving side scores a point.

13.3.1 After the service is returned, the shuttle is hit by either player of the serving side and then by either player of the receiving side, and so on, until the shuttle ceases to be in play.

13.3.2 After the service is returned, a player may hit the shuttle from any position on that player's side on the net.

13.4.1 If the receiving side makes a "fault" or the shuttle ceases to be in play because it touches the surface of the court inside the receiving side's court, the serving side scores a point, and the server serves again.

13.4.2 If the serving side makes a "fault" or the shuttle ceases to be in play because it touches the surface of the court inside the serving side's court, the server loses the right to continue serving, with no point scored by either side.

13.5.1 The player who serves at the start of any game shall serve from, or receive in, the right service court when that player's side has not scored or has scored an even number of points in that game, and the left service court otherwise.

13.5.2 The player who receives at the start of any game shall receive in, or serve from, the right service court when that player's side has not scored or has scored an even number of points in that game, and the left service court otherwise.

13.5.3 The reverse pattern applies to partners.

13.5.4 If a game is set, the total points scored by a side in that game shall be used to apply Laws 13.5.1 to 13.5.3.

13.6 Service in any turn of serving shall be delivered from alternate service courts, except as provided in Laws 14 and 16.

13.7 The right to serve passes consecutively from the initial server in any game to the initial receiver in that game, and then consecutively from that player to that player's partner and then to one of the opponents and then the opponent's partner, and so on.

13.8 No player shall serve out of turn, receive out of turn, or receive two consecutive services in the same game, except as provided in Laws 14 and 16.

13.9 Either player of the winning side may serve first in the next game and either player of the losing side may receive.

14. SERVICE COURT ERRORS

14.1 A service court error has been made when a player:
14.1.1 Has served out of turn;
14.1.2 Has served from the wrong service court; or
14.1.3 Standing in the wrong service court, was prepared to receive the service and it has been delivered.

14.2 When a service court error has been made, then:

    14.2.1 If the error is discovered before the next service is delivered, it is a "let" unless only one side was at fault and lost the rally, in which case the error shall not be corrected.

    14.2.2 If the error is not discovered before the next service is delivered, the error shall not be corrected.

14.3 If there is "let" because of a service court error, the rally is replayed with the error corrected.

14.4 If a service court error is not to be corrected, play in that game shall proceed without changing the players' new service courts (nor, when relevant, the new order of serving).

15. FAULTS

It is a "fault":

15.1 If a service is not correct (Law 11.1);

15.2 If the server, in attempting to serve, misses the shuttle;

15.3 If after passing over the net on service, the shuttle is caught in or on the net;

15.4 If in play, the shuttle:

    15.4.1 Lands outside the boundaries of the court;

    15.4.2 Passes through or under the net;

    15.4.3 Fails to pass the net;

    15.4.4 Touches the roof, ceiling, or side walls;

    15.4.5 Touches the person or dress of a player; or

    15.4.6 Touches any other object or person outside the immediate surroundings of the court; (Where necessary, on account of the structure of the building, the local badminton authority may, subject to the right of veto of its National Organization, make by-laws dealing with cases in which a shuttle touches an obstruction.)

15.5 If, when in play, the initial point of contact with the shuttle is not on the striker's side of the net. (The striker may, however, follow the shuttle over the net with the racquet in the course of a stroke.)

15.6 If, when the shuttle is in play, a player:

    15.6.1 Touches the net or its supports with racquet, person or dress;

    15.6.2 Invades an opponent's court OVER THE NET with racquet or person except as permitted in Law 15.5;

15.6.3 Invades an opponent's court UNDER THE NET with racquet or person such that an opponent is obstructed or distracted; or

15.6.4 Obstructs an opponent, i.e. prevents an opponent from making a legal stroke where the shuttle is followed over the net;

15.7 If, in play, a player deliberately distracts an opponent by any action such as shouting or making gestures;

15.8 If, in play, the shuttle:

15.8.1 Be caught and held on the racquet and slung during the execution of a stroke;

15.8.2 Be hit twice in succession by the same player with two strokes (a double hit by one player with one stroke is not a fault); or

15.8.3 Be hit by a player and the player's partner successively; or

15.8.4 Touches a player's racquet and continues toward the back of that player's court.

15.9 If a player is guilty of flagrant, repeated or persistent offenses under Law 18.

16. LETS

"Let" is called by the Umpire, or by a player (if there is no Umpire) to halt play.

16.1 A "let" may be given for any unforeseen or accidental occurrence.

16.2 If a shuttle, after passing over the net, is caught in or on the net, it is a "let" except during service.

16.3 If during service, the receiver and server are both faulted at the same time, it shall be a "let."

16.4 If the server serves before the receiver is ready, it shall be a "let."

16.5 If during play, the shuttle disintegrates and the base completely separates from the rest of the shuttle, it shall be a "let."

16.6 If a Line Judge is unsighted and the Umpire is unable to make a decision, it shall be a "let."

16.7 When a "let" occurs, the play since the last service shall not count, and the player who served shall serve again, except when Law 14 is applicable.

17. SHUTTLE NOT IN PLAY

A shuttle is not in play when:

17.1 It strikes the net and remains attached there or suspended on top;

17.2 It strikes the net or post and starts to fall towards the surface of the court on the striker's side of the net;

17.3   It hits the surface of the court; or

17.4   A "fault" or "let" has occurred.

18. CONTINUOUS PLAY, MISCONDUCT, PENALTIES

18.1   Play shall be continuous from the first service until the match is concluded, except as allowed in Laws 18.2 and 18.3.

18.2   An interval not exceeding 5 minutes is allowed between the second and third games of all matches in all of the following situations:

   18.2.1 In international competitive events;

   18.2.2 In IBF sanctioned events; and

   18.2.3 In all other matches (unless the National Organization has previously published a decision not to allow such an interval).

18.3   When necessitated by circumstances not within the control of the players, the Umpire may suspend play for such a period as the Umpire may consider necessary. If play be suspended, the existing score shall stand and play be resumed from that point.

18.4   Under no circumstances shall play be suspended to enable a player to recover his strength or wind, or to receive instruction or advice.

   18.5.1 Except in the intervals provided in Laws 18.2 and 18.3, no player shall be permitted to receive advice during a match.

   18.5.2 Except at the conclusion of a match, no player shall leave the court without the Umpire's consent.

18.6   The Umpire shall be the sole judge of any suspension of play.

18.7   A player shall not:

   18.7.1 Deliberately cause suspension of play;

   18.7.2 Deliberately interfere with the speed of the shuttle;

   18.7.3 Behave in an offensive manner; or

   18.7.4 Be guilty of misconduct not otherwise covered by the Laws of Badminton.

18.8   The Umpire shall administer any breach of Law 18.4, 18.5, or 18.7 by:

   18.8.1 Issuing a warning to the offending side;

   18.8.2 Faulting the offending side, if previously warned; or

   18.8.3 In cases of flagrant offense or persisting offenses, faulting the offending side and reporting the offending side immediately to the Referee, who shall have the power to disqualify.

18.9   Where a referee has not been appointed, the responsible official shall have the power to disqualify.

19. OFFICIAL AND APPEALS

19.1 The Referee is in overall charge of the tournament or event of which a match forms part.

19.2 The Umpire, where appointed, is in charge of the match, the court and its immediate surrounds. The Umpire shall report to the Referee. In the absence of a Referee, the Umpire shall report instead to the responsible official.

19.3 The Service Judge shall call service faults made by the server should they occur (Law 11).

19.4 A Line Judge shall indicate whether a shuttle is "in" or "out".

AN UMPIRE SHALL:

19.5 Uphold and enforce the Laws of Badminton and, especially call a "fault" or "let" should either occur, without appeal being made by the players;

19.6 Give a decision on any appeal regarding a point of dispute, if made before the next service is delivered;

19.7 Ensure players and spectators are kept informed of the progress of the match;

19.8 Appoint or remove Line Judges or a Service Judge in consultation with the Referee;

19.9 Not overrule the decision of Line Judges and the Service Judge on points of fact;

    19.10.1 Where another court official is not appointed, arrange for their duties to be carried out;

    19.10.2 Where an appointed official is unsighted, carry out the official's duties or play a "let";

19.11 Decide upon any suspension of play;

19.12 Record and report to the Referee all matters in relation to Law 18; and

19.13 Take to the Referee all unsatisfied appeals on questions of law only. (Such appeals must be made before the next service is delivered, or, if at the end of a game, before the side that appeals has left the court.)

BADMINTON STRATEGY

Badminton is a fast-paced game that calls for a good combination of skill and strategy. The basic strategy is simple, with two main objectives. Your strategy should be to move your opponent into a position that allows you to make attacking shots as often as possible. Conversely, you need to prevent yourself from being moved into positions that provide your opponent with the opportunity to make attacking shots into your court. Skilled badminton players can quickly discern whether an incoming shot will permit for an attacking return or a defensive return, executes the correct shot into the best aiming area in the opponent's court, and then moves into the correct position in anticipation of the opponent's return. The sequence of: (1) recognizing the incoming shot, (2) selecting and hitting the most appropriate shot to the opponent, and (3) moving and anticipating the opponent's return, forms the most basic pattern in badminton strategy.

SERVING STRATEGY

1. Use a variety of serves with an unpredictable pattern and placement.
2. In most cases, it is preferable to serve to your opponent's backhand side.
3. The high deep serve is usually most effective against other beginner players (preferably to your opponent's backhand side).
4. Force your opponent into a defensive return by placements to the extreme front and back corners.
5. Learn to make all serves from the same spot and with the same basic motion. This will prevent your opponent from being tipped off by pre-serving changes.
6. Immediately return to the middle of your court, in the ready position, once the shuttle has crossed the net into your opponent's court.
7. From the ready position, anticipate your opponent's return shot and be ready to move in that direction. Do not leave middle court too soon, however!

SERVICE RETURN STRATEGY

1. Work to develop skills in returning all types of serves. Do not be vulnerable to a certain kind of serve.
2. Set up in the ready position in the middle of the service return box. Do not "shade" or "lean" to favor any one direction. Remember, you can't move while the serve is being made.

3. In most cases you will get a serve that dictates a defensive return by you. Do not force an attacking return when one is not clearly available.
4. If possible, return the serve with a clear to your opponent's back boundary and move into the middle of your court in the ready position, anticipating an attacking opportunity on your next shot.

RALLY STRATEGY (SINGLES)

1. Badminton is a game of positioning and shot placement. Try to stay in the middle of your court and have a definite purpose and aiming area for every shot you make. Do not "just hit it back and forth."
2. Do not force attacking opportunities. Be patient by hitting defensive shots until an attacking opportunity comes—and then attack hard!
3. Control your opponent's moves by using a variety of shots into different aiming areas. Do not let your opponent hit shots from his or her middle court area.
4. Try a variety of shots in the beginning of a match to search for a vulnerability. Once you have found it, hit that shot when you need "big" points.
5. Use shots that move your opponent into the extreme corners of the court. If he or she makes a mistake on a return, you will have more open court to aim at for your attacking shot.

SERVING POSITION FOR DOUBLES

In doubles the serving player must stand in the appropriate box, according to the score at the time. His or her partner must stand in the other serving box. The rules allow the nonserving player to stand anywhere in that box, but strategically it is best to stand in the back-middle (see Photo 8.1).

RALLY STRATEGY (DOUBLES)

Two basic formations are used in doubles play: side by side and back and front. In side by side, the court is divided into right and left territories by the center line. Each partner is assigned one side as a way of determining who will

Photo 8.1
Serving positions for doubles

return shots to that side. This formation works best when one partner is stronger than the other on backhand shots (the stronger player takes the left side). See Photo 8.2. In back and front, the court is divided into front and back territories by an imaginary line. This formation is used when one part-ner is quicker or has better racquet control (front) and one partner is stronger (back). See Photo 8.3. Communication and experience with each other are the keys for both formations.

1. The action in doubles is much quicker than in singles, so shot selection is critical.
2. Look for attack opportunities more quickly than in singles.
3. Aim attacks to an opponent's body, rather than a court area.
4. Avoid cross-court attacks that leave large open areas for return attacks.
5. Be decisive with shot selection and aiming areas. Your opponents have two chances to return misplaced shots!

Photo 8.2
Side by side for doubles

Photo 8.3
Back and front for doubles

BADMINTON KNOWLEDGE AND STRATEGY QUIZ

Your name _____

Circle (T)rue or (F)alse for each statement.

1. T   F   Either side can score points in badminton.

2. T   F   The side winning the last game serves first in the next game.

3. T   F   It is legal for the server to have one foot completely out of the designated serving area.

4. T   F   A fault is scored when the server misses hitting the shuttle on an attempted serve.

5. T   F   In singles think "defense first, attack second" and in doubles think "attack first, defense second."

6. T   F   If a service court error is not discovered before the next serve is delivered, the previous serves stands.

7. T   F   It is legal to make initial contact with the shuttle on your side of the net and follow through over (but not touching) the net.

8. T   F   The head of the racquet does not have to be completely below the server's racquet hand when the shuttle is struck to be legal.

9. T   F   Once you find an opponent's vulnerability, keep hitting your shots to that weakness until he or she makes an adjustment.

10. T   F   In a singles match, the server has 4 points. Her or his next serve will come from the left service box.

11. T   F   "Setting" is similar to a tie-breaker in tennis.

12. T   F   The player or team reaching the designated score second has the option of setting.

13. T   F   You hit an accurate drive clear to your opponent. She or he will likely return with a defensive shot, and you can prepare for an attack.

14. T   F   A shuttle that hits a box line or a boundary line is considered "good."

15. T   F   If a game is set at 13-all, the first player or team to reach 15 wins the game.

16. T   F   Unless a game is set, all badminton games are to 15 points.

17. T   F   If both the server and the returner are moving when the shuttle is contacted, it is a let and the serve is replayed with no change in score.

18. T   F   In doubles, it is legal for a team to make consecutive contacts if the first contact was not with the racquet (that is the shuttle touched one player's body and was then hit by her or his partner).

19. T   F   It is good strategy to make several "false starts" when serving to disrupt your opponent's timing.

20. T   F   In doubles, the first serve of each side is always from the right service box.

Personal Progress Chart for PSIS Tennis

Module		Weeks in Class														
		1	2	3	4	5	6	7	8	9	10	11	12	13	14	15
8	Laws and Strategy															
7	Drop Shots															
6	Overhead Smashes															
5	Drive Shots															
4	Clears															
3	Serving															
2	Badminton Basics															
1	Stretching